Electoral Reform and Minority Representation

Electoral Reform and Minority Representation: Local Experiments with Alternative Elections

Shaun Bowler, Todd Donovan, and David Brockington

The Ohio State University Press
Columbus

Library of Congress Cataloging-in-Publication Data

Bowler, Shaun, 1958–
Electoral reform and minority representation : local experiments with alternative elections / Shaun Bowler, Todd Donovan, and David Brockington.
p. cm.
Includes bibliographical references and index.
ISBN 0-8142-0917-3 (hardcover : alk. paper)—ISBN 0-8142-9000-0 (CD-ROM)
1. Proportional representation—United States. 2. Voting—United States. 3. Election districts—United States. 4. Representative government and representation—United States. I. Donovan, Todd. II. Brockington, David. III. Title.
JF1075.U6 B69 2003
324.6′3′0973—dc21

2002015358

Text and jacket design by Sans Serif, Inc.
Type set in Times Roman by Sans Serif.
Printed by Thomson-Shore Inc.

The paper used in this publication meets the minimum requirements of the American National Standard for Information Sciences—Permanence of Paper for Printed Library Materials. ANSI Z39.48-1992.

9 8 7 6 5 4 3 2 1

CONTENTS

List of Tables and Figures vi

Acknowledgments ix

1. Minority Representation and Electoral System Reform 1

2. Cumulative Voting as an Alternative 14

3. The Strategic Demands of Cumulative and Limited Voting 32

4. Elite Response to Cumulative Voting Election Rules 39

5. Election Rules and Political Campaigns (with Tracy Sulkin) 51

6. Voter Response to Campaigns and New Election Rules 65

7. Alternative Electoral Rules and Voter Mobilization 75

8. Minority Representation under Alternative Electoral Arrangements 92

9. Conclusions about the Consequences of Minority Representation via Cumulative Voting (with Susan Banducci and Jeff Karp) 107

Appendixes 120

Notes 132

Bibliography 143

Index 157

LIST OF TABLES AND FIGURES

Figures

1.1. A Model of Election System Effects 11
2.1. Sample CV Ballot 24
2.2. Threshold of Exclusion by Number of Seats Contested under CV 27
2.3. Ballot Structure and Electoral Systems 30
4.1. Electoral System Change and Mobilization of Candidates: Morton Independent School District, Texas 40
4.2. Electoral System Change and Mobilization of Candidates: Peoria, Illinois, City Council 41
8.1. CV/LV Seats-Population Relationship Compared to Other Systems, U.S. South 100
8.2. CV/LV Seats-Population Relationship Compared to Other Systems, U.S. South 101

Tables

2.1. Partial List of Jurisdictions Adopting CV and LV in the United States 22
2.2. Cumulative and Limited Voting Arrangements in U.S. Communities 25
2.3. Thresholds of Representation and Exclusion under Plurality, CV, LV, D'Hondt, and Largest Remainder 26
3.1. Possible Vote Distributions for Two Voters and Their Consequences for the Vote Shares of Two Candidates (c1 and c2) under CV 33
3.2. Seats Won with Optimal Nominations under CV 38
4.1. Candidate Vote Apportionment Strategies in U.S. Local CV Elections 44
4.2. Endorsing Group Vote Apportionment Strategies in U.S. Local CV Elections 45
4.3. Group Mobilization Activity in U.S. Local CV and Plurality Elections 47
5.1. CV Candidate and Plurality Candidate Campaign Activity Compared 53
5.2. Percentage of Candidates without Challengers, by Election System 54

5.3. Estimations of Campaign Spending, by Election System (Dependent Variable = Dollars of Expenditure) 56
5.4. Factor Analysis of Candidate Campaign Activity 59
5.5. Estimations of Campaign "Style" (Dependent Variable = Factor Scores from Factor 1, Table 4) 60
5.6. Estimation of Group-Based Campaign Activity (Dependent Variable = Group Campaigned on Behalf of Candidate) 62
6.1. Voter Knowledge of CV Strategies, Sisseton, South Dakota 68
6.2. Voter Evaluations of CV Difficulty, Sisseton, South Dakota 68
6.3. New Voters' Evaluations of CV Difficulty, Sisseton, South Dakota 69
6.4. Voter Reports of Campaign Contacts and Requests for Plumping, by Racial Group of Voter 70
6.5. Plumping in Local CV Elections in the United States: Percentage of Minority Candidate's Votes Received by Type of Vote 71
6.6. Response to Mobilizing Effects of CV Election, Sisseton, South Dakota 74
7.1. Descriptive Characteristics: All Cases, Controls, and Experimental Groups 82
7.2. Cross-Sectional Models of Turnout in Local CV and LV Elections 85
7.3. Cross-Sectional Models of Turnout in Local CV Elections 86
7.4. Longitudinal Models of Turnout in Local CV Elections 88
8.1. Election of Minority Candidates under CV and LV 96
8.2. Minority Seats-Population Relationship under CV and LV 99
8.3. African American Seats—Population Relationship under CV and LV 102
8.4. Latino Representation under CV, Estimated by Population, Registration, and Relative Participation: Places with Latino Candidates 104
9.1. Effect of Minority Representation on Attitudes about Government Responsiveness, OLS Estimates 110
9.2. Effect of Minority Representation on Voting: Logistic Regression Estimates of Reported Participation in Elections 111

Appendixes

A. Communities Identified as Using CV or LV 120
B. Candidate Survey Methods (Chapters 4, 5, and 6) 123
C. Case Selection Methods: Turnout Data (Chapter 7) 126

D. Jurisdictions Included in Turnout Analysis as Matched Places (Chapter 7): Number of Election Cases Used in Models 2 and 3, Table 7.3 127
E. Case Selection Methods: Election Result Data (Chapter 8) 129
F. Jurisdictions Included in the Population-Seats Analysis (Models 1 and 2, Chapter 8) 130

ACKNOWLEDGMENTS

We would like to thank a number of people who helped us to accomplish and improve this project. Bob Brischetto, Dick Engstrom, and David Farrell gave us useful feedback on parts of the project in its various guises. Bernie Grofman read and made many helpful comments on the entire manuscript as did the anonymous reviewers for OSU Press. All of these people helped strengthen the manuscript. Dick Engstrom and Bob Brischetto also generously shared their survey data with us.

Research support came from the Academic Senate at UC Riverside and the WWU Bureau for faculty research. Tom Sykes, of the Washington State Institute for Public Policy, who funded the initial stages of research on this project. The Universiteit Twente, Netherlands also provided valuable support for us.

We would also like to thank a number of students who helped us along the way. Chapter 4 was co-written with Tracy Sulkin. Charles Malone and Elizabeth Cotrell of WWU and UCR students Helen Delgado, Jose Escoto, and Tim Paynich did a terrific job in helping gather the survey data.

As always, Malcolm Litchfield and the staff at OSU Press, especially Karie Kirkpatrick, did a wonderful job in moving the manuscript into the book you see now.

· 1 ·

Minority Representation and Electoral System Reform

In May of 2000 the city of Amarillo, Texas, held an election for its school board. Although the 24 percent of city residents are minority, only one minority candidate (a Latino) had ever been elected to its school board.[1] On the morning of May 8 the local newspaper, the *Globe-News,* highlighted the election of two members in particular—James Allen and Rita Sandoval, the board's first African American and Latina members. The newspaper report continued:

> While Allen stopped short of crediting the school district's new voting system for his victory, Alphonso Vaughn, president of the Amarillo chapter of the National Association for the Advancement of Colored People, said it is clear that minority voters used the system.
>
> "I think you have to say cumulative voting was a plus," Vaughn said. "It's the first time in the history of this area that two minorities were elected to the school board. That has never happened before, and I think cumulative voting had an effect on that." (*Amarillo Globe-News,* May 8, 2000)

Not only that, but voter turnout was higher than in previous years:

> Of the 96,716 registered voters in AISD, 12,280 (or 12.7 percent) cast ballots in this election. By comparison, only 3.4 percent of the registered voters turned out for the May 1998 election. (*Amarillo Globe-News,* May 8, 2000)

The main question posed by this project is a simple one: how general are these claims? Did the adoption of a new electoral system produce these outcomes—increased minority representation and higher turnout—or was it something specific to the city and Amarillo in that time[2] and that place?

In an era of changing demographics and low participation, if the switch to a new electoral system can really produce greater diversity in representation and higher turnout, then there might be something to be said for it. Moreover, the election was held in a census year—a year during which some of the redistricting battles spawned by the previous census had yet to be resolved (Engstrom 2000). If electoral reform could end some of these long and expensive legal battles, that, too, would be a plus.

A number of scholars, most notably, perhaps, Lani Guinier, could have said, on seeing the results from Amarillo, "I told you so." Over the years a number of advocates, including Guinier, have made the case in favor of electoral reform as a remedy for minority underrepresentation. In fact, many of the major arguments in favor of cumulative voting (CV) as a remedy have been known since the nineteenth century. In writings and speeches of U.S. Senator Charles Buckalew (1872), in nineteenth-century English school board elections, in the Illinois state legislature elections, or, even earlier, in elections for legislatures in Britain's Cape Colonies, CV was seen as a means to address minority rights; whether the relevant minority was partisan, religious, or a different nationality.

The modern context of minority representation in the United States means, of course, the representation of nonwhite Americans. According to the U.S. Census, in 1992 the nonwhite population of the United States was 25.2 percent. By 2000 it had reached 28.2 percent—12.2 percent African American, 11.4 percent Hispanic origin, and 3.9 percent Asian/Pacific Islander. Some minority groups have had relative success in gaining representation in large cities, in some state legislatures, and in Congress. In the mid-1990s, for example, after the use of race to draw safe minority districts, 14 percent of U.S. House members were nonwhite. These gains, however, detract from the fact that descriptive representation of minorities is lower at the local level. Of 419,716 local elected officials recorded by the U.S. Bureau of the Census in 1992, only 2.7 percent were black, and only 1.3 percent were Hispanic.[3] In most of the nation's representative bodies, minorities are largely shut out.[4]

It is hardly surprising, then, to find that several commentators and scholars have advocated electoral reform—typically either "majority-minority" districts or variants of proportional representation (PR)—as solutions to the underrepresentation of minorities on local councils and legislatures. And as we see below, some reformers have expectations for new election rules that go beyond simply achieving descriptive representation.

But reforms do not always live up to the claims of their advocates. Although advocates of a particular institutional reform—whether that reform is term limits, a balanced-budget amendment, or even, as in this case, electoral system reform—are quick to claim advantages of a given reform proposal, the disadvantages are often downplayed and the advantages often asserted rather than shown. This is especially the case with electoral system reform. Electoral engineers, and would-be electoral engineers, are often confident in their claims about the effects of systems, often on the basis of only one or two examples. After all, electoral reform, at least at the national level, remains a relatively rare event, so examples of change are often few and far between. To be sure, the study of electoral system design is one of the most advanced literatures in political science. Even so, claims concerning the efficacy of institutional reforms, such as changing the electoral system, may be overstated or mistaken.

In this project we put to test, for the first time, the claims made on behalf of CV in relation to minority representation. In doing so, we present one of the few studies of the impact of any electoral system reform that is based on scores rather than on a handful of cases. Consequently, we are able to state our conclusions with a greater degree of confidence than previous studies on the topic.

This study, then, combines two elements—a question concerning how one may demonstrate the effects of electoral system reform with a concern for one of the major, substantive political problems facing the United States in the new century—minority representation. We compare how minorities fare under local majoritarian systems (at large and districting) versus under "alternative" electoral systems. At issue here is how "alternative" election rules such as CV and limited voting (LV) might resolve problems involved with the representation of minorities in the United States.

In the chapters that follow, we demonstrate that local experiments with these "new" electoral systems have produced *more* minority representation in the United States than the majoritarian systems they replace. More importantly, however, we assess how CV and LV affect the process of elections and possibly produce minority representation *differently*—in ways that might be seen as normatively better than the standard local election methods used in the United States (at large or districting). We find that local elections contested under CV differ in important ways from those held under the rules they replace. Not only are more minorities elected, but CV elections may be more competitive, campaigns may be subtly more active, and turnout may be higher under CV than under majoritarian rules (including districting). The Amarillo case, it seems, may be a general example of how CV might change local politics after all.

Minority Representation in the United States

Minority representation is one of the thornier issues of democracy. At its simplest, democracy is a system of majority rule. Yet, if democracy is reduced to this single element it cannot survive. In practice, a functioning democracy must provide some institutionalized protections for minorities if it is to thrive. To recognize this, however, is to raise a series of questions: What role should minorities have in a democracy predicated on majority rule? Which minorities are at issue? How should their interests be incorporated in decision making? Most critically, how should the answers to these questions be institutionalized into the rules that structure the political system?

Constitutional engineers and political theorists have provided a variety of answers to such questions. In much of continental Europe, democratic systems have evolved what Arend Lijphart (1984) called "consensual" models of democracy, in which institutional rules (including PR) make it difficult for minority voices to be ignored at key points in the political process. Democracies that are heirs to the British system, however, have built institutions that are decidedly more "majoritarian" in the sense that agendas are built upon "winner-take-all" rules and are more easily dominated by a small number of broadly based parties or groups. One key difference between consensual and majoritarian systems is how electoral rules provide minority interests with influence.

For all the potential advantages of majoritarian electoral systems such as those in the United States, the United Kingdom, and Canada, the representation of minorities remains problematic. This is a particularly important issue for the United States, given the increasingly multicultural and multiracial nature of society. African Americans held about a 12 percent share of the population for much of the twentieth century. At the century's end, a highly diverse mix of Latinos claimed (nearly) as large a share, with an increasing number and equally diverse mix of Asians. Even in states where they have been concentrated for centuries (California, Florida, New York, Texas, and states in the South), it has been difficult for blacks and Latinos to win elections.

One of the primary barriers to representation for these groups is electoral rules. Under majoritarian rules, if white voters resist supporting nonwhite candidates (Reeves 1997), and nonwhite candidates run where most voters are white, the chances of a nonwhite's being elected are slim. In Amarillo, minority candidates had managed to get to the runoff stage several times in the previous "at-large" majoritarian system. Once there, however, they could rarely win (Rausch 2001).

Recognition of this problem led to the creation of homogeneous, "majority-minority" districts designed so that most residents come from a single racial or ethnic minority group (Grofman and Davidson 1992; Lublin 1997). Federal legislation and court rulings accelerated the process of creating such districts for the 1990 congressional reapportionment, leading to a large influx of minority representatives in the U.S. House of Representatives by 1992. Earlier challenges to plurality "at-large" rules common at the local level led to districting that also produced dramatic increases in minority representation in the 1970s and 1980s in cities with sizable minority populations (Welch 1990; Engstrom and McDonald 1981). In 1986, in *Thornburg v. Gingles,*[5] the Court ruled that "at-large" elections could present an unconstitutional dilution of minority vote strength in many situations. Thus, the remedy to vote dilution in local and federal elections has been to segregate racial and ethnic groups in homogeneous electorates where they may form a majority.

However, as we shall see in chapter 2, districting on the basis of race has come under increased criticism from U.S. courts. The *Shaw v. Reno* decision (1993)[6] criticized "bizarre"-shaped districts that can result from such efforts. When race is found to be the "predominant factor" in districting, the contemporary Supreme Court will make it extremely difficult for state and local governments to establish a compelling interest in adopting such districts.

In addition, observers note the practical and political issues associated with creating homogeneous districts in communities that are increasingly multicultural (Guinier 1994; Valadez 2001). Districting solutions become even more problematic when a jurisdiction's minority populations are spatially dispersed (which is more common outside of the South). In 1980, 14 percent of U.S. cities with over 100,000 residents had two or more nonwhite racial/ethnic groups that *each* made up at least 10 percent of the population. By 1990, 23 percent of cities had at least two nonwhite groups (including Asians, Hispanics, or blacks) making up at least 10 percent of the population (MacManus 1995, 42). It is highly likely that even more U.S. cities and towns became multicultural through the year 2000.

While plaintiffs were advancing minority representation via race-based districting, a few jurisdictions facing vote dilution lawsuits took a different tack. In the 1980s, Latino plaintiffs used the Supreme Court's *Gingles* criteria to successfully challenge the at-large election rules of Alamogordo, New Mexico. For various reasons—including a dispersed Latino population that made it difficult to draw majority Latino districts—plaintiffs and the city agreed to experiment with CV. Peoria, Illinois, also adopted CV in 1991 to allow African Americans to secure council seats in that city. By the 1990s, dozens of additional cities, towns, counties, school districts, and special districts in Alabama, Arizona, North Carolina, South Dakota, and Texas had conducted their own experiments with "alternatives" to districting. As we will see, under certain conditions, CV and a related system, LV, provide for minority representation at levels that rival those obtained via districting.[7] These "alternative" systems might be seen as halfway points between "winner-take-all" majoritarian rules and the proportional rules that are the basis of "consensual" democracies.

These relatively recent local innovations provide an opportunity to assess a number of critical questions, including how to bring about descriptive representation of minority voters. In crude terms, descriptive representation concerns how closely elected representatives look like the underlying population. One debate over minority representation in the United States concerns how many African American and Latino/Latina minorities should serve on elected bodies given the demographic makeup of an area. Important as this emphasis on descriptive accuracy is, it may not constitute the full range of concerns about what we expect from elections and, by extension, what we expect about representation. A singular emphasis on descriptive representation carries with it a concern for *outcomes* of elections almost to the exclusion of concerns about the *process* of elections. As we argue below, elections and electoral systems can have important effects on how candidates behave when they seek office and on how voters behave in response to this. Electoral system reform may change not only descriptive representation but also the conduct of elections, and this, too, ought to be considered.

Local experiments with these alternative electoral regimes allow us to look at more than just how different election rules produce different levels of minority representation. They also allow us to assess how different elections create incentives that affect whether candidates seek office, whether they will campaign actively, and how much they need to mobilize voters. In studying these local elections, then, we are able to ask important questions about the democratic process. Some of these raise practical issues about descriptive representation, while others take up conceptual questions about the importance of process in debates over representation. It is important to remember that *how* a community chooses its representatives may be just as important as *who* the representatives are.

Using Local Elections to Assess the Effects of Electoral Reform

These alternative attempts at providing minority representation give us an opportunity to look at the effects of electoral institutions in an ideal setting—U.S. local elections. Most research on electoral systems draws from national-level electoral experience in the major Western democracies. Local elections are generally regarded as "second-order" elections, mere sideshows to the main national elections. There are, however, important reasons to use these local elections to help us develop an understanding of electoral institutions and what they do.

Local elections are the most common kinds of elections that are held in the United States, yet we know very little about them. The fact that there are a large number of them means that they provide an ideal laboratory for the study of institutional change. Changes in electoral regime at the local level allow us to examine the effects of reform with better evidence (or, at least, more cases) than at the national level, where election rules rarely change. In the rare cases where established democracies do alter their elections, as with Italy (Katz 1996), New Zealand (Vowles et al. 1998; Banducci, Donovan, and Karp 1999), and Japan

(Christensen and Johnson 1995), a "before and after" comparison is possible. This single-case approach typically yields rich detail about the effects of reforms in each place. But inferences concerning the general effects of a reform are difficult to draw on the basis of just one or two examples.

There have been a series of studies that compare politics at a fixed point in time across nations that have been categorized by their electoral regime (e.g., Rae 1971; Lijphart 1994; Taagepera and Shugart 1989; Blais and Carty 1990; Jackman 1987; Powell 1986; Anderson and Guillory 1997). One theme to emerge from these studies is that proportional election rules provide greater representation of minorities, yield higher turnout, and may produce more positive attitudes about democratic politics.

As valuable as this work has been, the findings are essentially based upon the same set of twenty or so nations whose experiences and social fabric vary in many different ways. Some of that variation—social, cultural, historical—is highly correlated with their election system.[8] Differences in politics between each set of nations might flow from elections or from cultural differences that affect how trusting people are, their propensity to join civic associations, or their political socialization. With differences in elections and culture so closely linked, statistics alone cannot neatly resolve if one (or both) are the causal force generating observed differences.

These issues are particularly problematic because one explanation of higher rates of voter participation is that some nations have distinctive "political cultures" that affect their citizens' "subjective orientation to politics" (Verba 1965, 513). If election rules covary with place-specific factors like culture, cross-national studies cannot be seen as definitive demonstrations of election rule effects. Ideally, we would test for the effect of election rules where political culture and social demographics are largely held constant.

Since nearly 100 U.S. jurisdictions have adopted CV and LV elections, we can expand the number of cases in our analysis well beyond the number of industrialized democracies. Moreover, we can compare the politics of these communities to other U.S. places that are nearly identical on a range of demographics—most notably ethnic composition, region, median education, and income levels. Our careful method of case selection allows us to compare places that have been "treated" with CV election rules (e.g., Peoria, Illinois) to "control" jurisdictions using majoritarian rules that are virtually identical on all other accounts (e.g., Rockford, Illinois). The major difference between each set of communities is that one uses "alternative" election rules while the other uses "winner-take-all" rules.

This is not to deny the differences that exist between places like Peoria and Rockford, Illinois. But demographic and cultural differences between two cities within the same region of a state are likely to be much shallower than differences across nations. This is not to say that the cross-national literature is wrong or misguided. Rather, we argue that our approach means that the findings of electoral system effects are less susceptible to the rival claims of "cultural effects" than findings from cross-national studies.

The practical electoral experiments going on in these U.S. communities thus provide us with a unique opportunity for conducting political research. We are in a position here to observe the effect of new institutions in a large number of places. The local setting also allows us the opportunity to compare what we observe in these places to a very similar set of cases that maintain different institutions. Short of being able to invent and clone a large number of polities where social and cultural factors are made constant across all cases, this is about as close to an experimental research setting as social scientists might hope to find for those who study the effects of election rules.

Looking beyond Outcomes to the Effects of Process

As noted above, we examine how various election processes might produce outcomes differently, if not produce the same outcomes "better." One assumption behind this line of inquiry is that institutional processes shape how candidates and voters behave.

Existing studies of electoral systems have not really examined how institutions affect individual-level behavior.[9] To some extent there may be little need to pay too much attention to the micro-level effects of election rules. After all, one of the main findings of election systems research is that election rules can shape outcomes in ways that are not necessarily dependent on how candidates or voters behave. One example is the link between proportionality and district magnitude: where more seats are elected, outcomes are more proportionate. This relationship may depend as much on simple arithmetic as on voter behavior or candidate action.[10] Yet, it may also be the case that many "mechanical" outcomes we attribute to election rules, such as fractionalization and turnout levels, are brought about by elite and voter responses to the rules that structure how campaigns are conducted (e.g., Gunther 1989; Cox 1997).

We know, for example, that electoral processes and outcomes shape voter attitudes. Citizens in PR systems feel more efficacious than those in places with majoritarian systems (Anderson and Guillory 1997; Banducci, Karp, and Donovan 1997), and there is evidence that minority citizens are more politically efficacious when they are "empowered" by the presence of a minority elected official (Bobo and Gilliam 1990).

Election rules also shape the incentives of political elites. These elites should, in principle, change or modify their behavior in line with incentives associated with various electoral arrangements (Cox 1997). It is this elite behavior that, in many instances, affects voter behavior and mediates the impact of electoral arrangements. That is, voters may respond not just to the immediate incentives of a particular system—such as the prospects that it might produce descriptive representation of their group—but also to the activities of parties, political organizations, and candidates who respond to the opportunities that election rules create. Although electoral systems can be engineered to produce different sorts of outcomes, they do so by altering underlying political processes—namely, the incentives that affect decisions elites make about contesting elections, campaigning for office, and responding to constituents (Bowler, Farrell, and McAllister 1996; Studlar and McAllister 1994; Bean 1990; Cain, Ferejohn, and Fiorina 1984).

To assume, for example, that PR or CV leads directly to greater efficacy or higher mass participation would suggest a sort of invisible hand that guides citizens to a realization of the potential outcomes that election rules create. But there is no invisible hand. Rather, elections show the very visible hand of groups, parties, and candidates at work, and changes in election rules affect how they mobilize and contest elections (Donovan 2001). This in turn affects how campaigns will be conducted, which in turn affects how voters might be mobilized by a campaign. Hence, we look at how (or if) candidates contest elections under various rules and what their campaigns are like.

These issues are often major concerns when electoral rules are reformed. Prominent examples include the adoption of race-conscious districting in the United States, the recommendation by the New Zealand Royal Commission on Electoral Reform (1986) of changes that led to the adoption of a mixed-member proportional (MMP) system, and the recommendations produced by the Jenkins Report (1998) in England about increasing the proportionality of plurality elections. Although the New Zealand study in particular includes discussion of how new rules might improve civic life, the impetus for reforms and the concerns of politicians who accept reforms obviously center on who wins and who loses under new rules.

The answer to the question "Who won?" clearly matters, especially when it involves questions of fairness. We take up this question in chapter 8. But democratic theorists also value participation in and of itself. This was especially important to Pateman (1970) and, even earlier, to John Stuart Mill. Current scholarship on deliberative democracy also views taking part in discussion and argument as a central component of the democratic process (Fishkin 1991). Pitkin (1967) and Birch (1971) noted the importance of process alongside the importance of outcome. As we shall see in this book, different election rules can produce very similar results in terms of outcomes yet provide very distinct effects on civic life. Thus, we need to ask not only "Who won?" but also "How did they win?"

Elections and Descriptive Representation of Minorities

In the chapters that follow, we provide a chain of presentation that links election rules, candidates, and voters to election outcomes—namely, the descriptive representation of ethnic and racial minorities. Descriptive representation means that "representatives are in their own persons and lives in some sense typical of the larger class of persons whom they represent. Black legislators represent Black constituents, women legislators represent women constituents, and so on" (Mansbridge 1999, 629).

Discussions of descriptive representation in empirical literature tend to pay little attention to the complexities hidden underneath this sweeping term. Yet a whole series of practical and conceptual problems underpin the idea of descriptive representation. For example, which groups need "describing" is often assumed by electoral engineers rather than arrived at by voters themselves. Deciding which groups are to be represented may be no easy matter to decide—numbers alone may not be a criterion.[11] Mansbridge (1999) noted that descriptive representation is a complex idea that is best applied in specific historic contexts—particularly those where institutional rules and political processes have at some point denied a minority group access to participation or representation.

In the United States, such denial of access includes racially polarized voting, barriers to registration, and at-large local elections that allow whites to sweep all seats. As noted, majority-minority districting is the main tool used in the United States to compensate for some of these barriers. Many nations use tools that are equally if not more explicit in their aims. Some set aside seats for specific religious, ethnic, occupational, or linguistic groups. Some maintain exclusive voting rolls for the election of indigenous people. Some nation's parties place quotas in party rules regarding the distribution of places on the party's candidate lists.

However, institutionalized electoral arrangements that advantage one group rather than another can have little ability to respond to changing demographics. Immigration, social and economic change, differential birth rates, and a host of other forces can lead to new claims from groups seeking descriptive representation. Single-member districts (SMDs), furthermore, can make it difficult for voters to express preferences for a "descriptive" representative when they have multiple interests (e.g., being a minority and a woman, or a Latina environmentalist).

Descriptive representation predetermined by election rules also raises a set of uncomfortably complicated practical questions and issues that are not easy to resolve. As Lani Guinier and other observers have asked: Will such elections be competitive? Will citizens be mobilized to participate? Can it be assumed that demographic traits (e.g., race) covary with political interests and values? In the chapters that follow, we answer some of these questions directly and some indirectly. We do this by studying both elite and mass behavior in the United States under different election systems and under different forms of representation. Since elite behavior constitutes a large part of the process of representation, our study of the effects of election rules has implications for normative ideas of representation. It is important, for example, to know if candidates campaign more actively under one system or another, as this might reflect how they perceive their constituents. Yet few discussions of electoral systems consider these kinds of trade-offs.

Plan of the Book

Figure 1.1 sums up the overall argument of the book. It maps, from left to right, the order that we examine the effects of election systems. The figure illustrates that election outcomes occur after the end of a chain of important events and that outcomes depend, in part, on how rules affect what candidates and groups do before votes are cast. Figure 1.1 does not represent a causal model that we plan on estimating in a single grand equation. Rather, it can be seen as a delineation of the ways in which election rules shape political life. Our purpose is to establish the relationships depicted at each stage of the process and to see how they are linked to the use of a specific electoral system.

In the next chapter, we provide a full discussion of how CV and LV elections work and offer an overview of their contemporary and historic use. In chapter 3, we illustrate how these elections produce a set of incentives, or strategic burdens, that candidates and groups must overcome in order to win. The material in chapter 3 may seem a bit technical to some readers, who may wish to skip ahead to the main empirical chapters. The major point of chapter 3 is that CV and LV require substantial coordination of elite and mass activity in order to produce proportional descriptive representation of minorities—more so than SMD plurality rules and more than list-PR rules. Thus, even though in principle CV may

FIGURE 1.1. A Model of Election System Effects

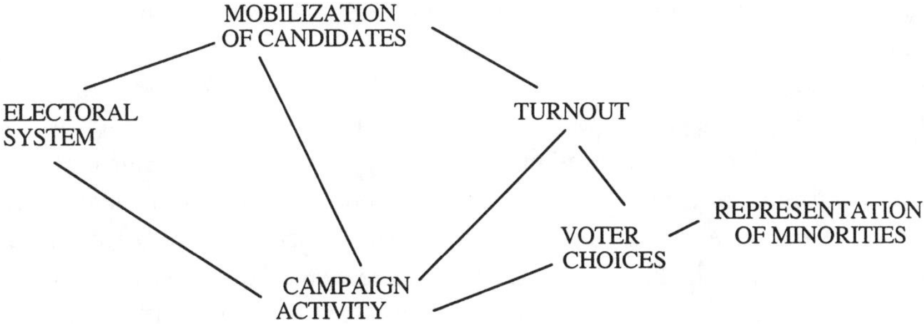

offer promise to minorities, in practice representation can come only after the strategic burdens of these election systems are overcome. As we see in the empirical chapters, however, minority candidates and organizations respond to these burdens in ways that might subtly invigorate political life in jurisdictions that use CV or LV.

The main empirical section of the book begins with chapter 4, where we look at elite behavior and assess whether, and how, candidates or groups respond to incentives and demands created by CV. Since nearly all CV elections are nonpartisan, it would seem that the deck is stacked against having political organizations available that can solve the coordination problems. As we see, however, minority political organizations "learn" how to contest CV, even in small jurisdictions conducting low-salience elections. We demonstrate that the adoption of CV leads to recruitment of more candidates, and we find groups working on behalf of minority candidates to register voters for CV elections. These candidates and groups also attempt to coordinate mass behavior under CV and thus can be seen responding to the strategic demands associated with CV.

In chapter 5, we take advantage of our comparative design and begin to assess how campaign activity under CV compares to campaign activity in similar places using at-large and districted elections. To do this, we surveyed candidates seeking office in CV and highly similar non-CV elections. We find substantial differences in the level of campaign activity, and the type of campaign activities, that candidates practice under different election rules. When compared to candidates in districted places, CV candidates appear to campaign more actively and are more likely to have organizations of some sort assisting their campaigns.

Following this, we look at voter response to CV campaigns. We assess how voters respond to the demands of ordinal election rules in chapter 6 and examine whether the vote coordination strategies transmitted by campaigns reach voters. Since our argument is that the effect of electoral institutions on voting behavior is mediated by the behavior of elites, we need to be able to show that voters are able to respond to the demands of novel electoral systems such as CV. If voters are unable or unwilling to respond, this seriously undercuts the overall argument. Here we rely on results from several CV contests and exit poll data from one CV election to test whether voters adopt the vote dispersion strategies required to produce minority representation.

Chapters 4, 5, and 6 thus provide assessments of the micro-level effects of CV elections on the process of campaigns and candidate activity. From here we examine the effects of CV election rules, and by implication CV campaigns, on the mobilization of voters. We ask if voters are more willing to turn out and vote under alternative electoral rules than under majoritarian rules. In chapter 7 we estimate how the adoption of new CV rules increases turnout in local U.S. elections. Moreover, we employ our comparative research design to illustrate how turnout differs between CV places and similar jurisdictions using standard plurality elections. We find that CV is associated with a significant increase in turnout in local elections.

Given that these new election rules were introduced with the intent of producing descriptive representation of minorities, it seems sensible to see if the changes had the desired effect. That is, do more minorities get into office once CV is adopted? Our answer in chapter 8 is that yes, they do. We find that minorities can gain representation under CV and LV in places where majoritarian/plurality rules have historically prevented them from winning seats. We demonstrate that in many practical settings CV and LV elections can produce the same representation of racial minorities as SMD plans. The potential for minority representation, however, depends upon how CV plans are designed, and a crucial issue here is the question of district magnitude. CV can ensure minority representation, but this may be contingent upon the number of seats up for election. Many CV plans in the United States have been implemented with too few seats at stake in a single election. This limits opportunities for minority representation. Yet even with these limitations, we see an increase in the number of minorities running for office and also winning under CV.

In our concluding chapter, we discuss some of the subtle attitudinal benefits of minority representation generally. We then assess the specific advantages of using CV to allow minority representation in a multicultural society. As noted above, minority representation is expected to have positive effects on the political attitudes of those being represented. We find that this is the case. Using survey data, we look at how white and nonwhite citizens respond to descriptive representation of minorities in Congress. We find that African Americans represented by an African American feel that government is more responsive and are more likely to vote than African Americans who have a white representative. At the same time, whites show no negative reaction to representation by nonwhites. We argue that CV can offer this same effect while producing additional effects that contribute to a well-functioning democracy: contested elections, active campaigns, and a mobilized electorate. It does this, moreover, in a way that lets groups organize themselves politically on the basis of their self-perceived (rather than institutionalized) interests. To put things bluntly, CV elections seem to work rather well.

Before beginning our discussion of the empirical work that leads us to this conclusion, we provide an account of how conflicts over minority representation in the United States have inched toward experiments with alternative electoral arrangements. It is to this we turn in the next chapter.

· 2 ·

Cumulative Voting as an Alternative

Nearly all elections in the United States are conducted under "winner-take-all" rules. For executive and legislative positions at the state and federal levels, all U.S. elections are variants on single-member simple-plurality (SMSP) rules. At the local level it is quite common for councils and school boards to be elected from multimember districts "at large," and some state legislatures have positions elected from multimember districts (Rule 1992; Conway 1992). Nevertheless, in all state-level elections using multimember districts, and in virtually all local cases, votes are translated into seats with majoritarian/plurality rules.

Despite the uniformity of majoritarian elections in the United States, there have been periods of experimentation with proportional elections at the local level. The origins and results of these experiments, sadly, have not been well studied. Leon Weaver (1984; 1986) documented that Populists, Progressives, and labor forces in several cities successfully advocated adoption of variants of proportional representation (PR) such as the single transferable vote (STV) early in the twentieth century.[1] Adoption of PR was promoted, in many instances, not with the goal of creating multiparty systems, but in order to break up one-party monopolies. Use of STV/PR was also relatively widespread in Ohio (Barber 1995; 2000) and in about two dozen medium and large cities, including Boulder, Colorado; Cincinnati, Cleveland, and Toledo, Ohio; Coos Bay, Oregon; Lowell, Massachusetts; Kalamazoo, Michigan; Sacramento, California; and New York City. Limited voting (LV) systems, which have the potential for "semiproportional" outcomes, are also used for at-large local elections in Connecticut and to elect most county commissions in Connecticut (Weaver 1984, 210).

At the middle of the century, a number of U.S. cities were continuing to use STV, including Cincinnati and Hopkins, Minnesota, which quit using STV in the 1960s. Cambridge, Massachusetts, uses STV to this day. Cincinnati returned to majoritarian rules in 1957 when an African American candidate was poised to become mayor (Engstrom 1993, 797). New York similarly returned to majoritarian elections for their city council after Communists were elected in 1940s (Zeller and Bone 1948). At the end of the twentieth century, New York City's community schools boards began using STV to facilitate representation in a highly multicultural setting. Although New York's school election system was the source of bitter legal fights, a 1999 Department of Justice ruling concluded that the system was effective in facilitating minority representation. After a lengthy review of STV in New York, the Department of Justice refused to preclear a law that would have replaced STV with LV.

America's brief flirtations with PR illustrate two interrelated issues: arguments about electoral arrangements are highly charged, and different rules create new winners and losers.

The Rise of "Majority-Minority" Districting in the United States

After most of these experiments with PR were long forgotten, concerns about the underrepresentation of racial and ethnic minorities spawned vigorous and successful challenges to certain aspects of U.S. plurality election rules. It should not seem surprising, then, that academic debates in the United States over the impact of electoral systems have been matched by a "real-world" and often highly contentious interest in the representation of ethnic and racial minorities. At-large elections at the local level, and even certain districting schemes used to elect legislatures, have been found to dilute the influence of minority voters.

By and large, the remedies used to facilitate minority representation have been further applications of winner-take-all rules in the form of drawing districts where minority voters hold a majority population share. The effects of majoritarian/plurality plans on representation, unlike the effects of the United States's brief experiments with PR, have been well established (see especially Davidson and Grofman 1994; Bullock 1994; Grofman and Davidson 1992).

A series of laws, court cases, lawsuits, and bitter political fights took place over these issues during the last several decades. The landmark 1965 Voting Rights Act (VRA) included key sections granting plaintiffs power to challenge local, state, and federal election plans that prevented blacks from voting. Section 5 of the original act required most jurisdictions in the South, and in some northern cities, to have any changes in election rules "precleared" by the Justice Department to ensure that the rules did not discriminate against black participation. In 1969 a landmark Supreme Court interpretation of the VRA allowed the Justice Department to also evaluate whether at-large election rules "diluted" the "effectiveness" of minority votes (*Allen v. Alabama State Elections Board*).[2] In 1975, Congress amended the VRA to extend to Latinos (as language minorities) standing to challenge election plans on such grounds. At one time, Section 5 preclearance applied to parts of twenty-two states (Davidson 1994, 31). During this era, lawsuits forced numerous local jurisdictions having few or no minority representatives to change from plurality at-large to plurality single-member district (SMD) plans, and black and Latino representation began to increase. State compliance with the VRA during the 1980 reapportionment of congressional delegations also led to an increase in House members elected from majority-minority districts in 1982.

Congress further amended Section 2 of the VRA in 1982 to define criteria that explicitly prohibited voting schemes resulting in minorities' having less opportunity than other voters to elect representatives of their choice (Davidson 1994, 35). The U.S. Supreme Court and circuit (appellate) court interpretations of challenges filed under the amended Section 2 further clarified the ability of plaintiffs to challenge local election plans that might dilute minority vote strength. In practice, plaintiffs needed to establish that they formed a cohesive political group, that white voters voted as block against minority candidates to deny them representation, and, in most instances, that the minority group could form a majority in a distinct geographic area in the jurisdiction (*Thornburg v. Gingles* 1986).

By the late 1980s, Latino plaintiffs filed successful challenges to at-large election plans outside the South, forcing the adoption of new district elections (*Gomez v. Watsonville* 1988; *Garza v. Los Angeles County* 1990).[3] Empowered with Section 2 and the Supreme Court's rulings, the Bush administration Justice Department and advocates of minority registration in many states pushed vigorously for a sharp increase in the number of U.S. House districts having a majority of minority voters during the 1990 reapportionments. This led to a record influx of African American and Latino House members in 1992.

The plans most often subject to challenge were councils elected under multimember at-large systems, although challenges to district plans that potentially diluted prospects for minority representation were not uncommon. It is hardly surprising that at-large local arrangements attracted particular attention. Although often viewed as part of "good government" reforms of the Progressive era, at-large elections often replaced districting plans with the intent of getting working-class ethnics, socialists, and blacks off city councils (Bridges 1997; Davidson and Korbel 1981; Hays 1964, 162). In these systems, where winners were elected by simple plurality, a jurisdiction-wide majority could determine the winner for every council position simultaneously. An at-large jurisdiction might divide the entire community into nominal districts or "positions" but at the same time allow all voters in the jurisdiction to elect each position by plurality or majority vote. A minority group with a 49 percent population share could conceivably vote as a block for a single minority candidate running for each position and be defeated every time.[4] This gave any reasonably cohesive majority group the power to sweep all positions elected under at-large rules.

The standard remedy in these situations has been changing to SMD plans, with districts drawn to facilitate minority representation. Although there is some controversy in the empirical literature about how minority representation might be best achieved via districting (Grofman and Handley 1989; Lublin 1997) it has been well established that African Americans and Latinos are more likely to win seats under single-member rules than under multimember at-large plans and that they are more likely to win seats from "majority-minority" districts. Indeed, a substantial body of evidence demonstrates that racial and ethnic minorities are more likely to win seats proportionate to their share of the population in districted jurisdictions (Bullock 1994; Polinard, Wrinkle, and Longoria, 1991; Welch 1990; Helig and Mundt 1983; Engstrom and McDonald 1981). Three decades of legislation, litigation, and electoral engineering had thus increased minority representation at all levels dramatically by the year 2000.

Challenges to Majority-Minority Districting as a Basis for Minority Representation

Districting on the basis of race, however, came under increased scrutiny by the courts in the 1990s. The *Shaw v. Reno* (1993) decision criticized "bizarre"-shaped districts.[5] *Miller v. Johnson* (1995) found a majority-minority congressional district unconstitutional and argued that districts should not be drawn on the basis of "race in substantial disregard of customary and traditional districting practices," such as protecting incumbents.[6] *Shaw v. Hunt* (1996) and *Bush v. Vera* (1996) found separate state congressional districting plans in violation of the Fourteenth Amendment's equal protection clause.[7] The contemporary Supreme Court has said that when race is found to be the "predominant factor" in districting, the court will apply the strict scrutiny test for the equal protection clause. This makes it extremely difficult for state and local governments to establish a compelling interest in adopting such districts in the future.

Critics of majority-minority districting have been raising additional concerns for decades. These include technical, political, and normative objections. As a practical matter, districting as a remedy for minority underrepresentation disadvantages minorities that are dispersed spatially, a situation not uncommon in jurisdictions with large Latino populations. This problem grows for any group as residential integration increases. Additional practical problems include knowing where to set the threshold for the concentration of minority voters into districts. In areas with a number of immigrants there can be extremely large disparities between the overall minority population and those who may vote. This makes it difficult to calculate the threshold needed to elect minority representatives. Even in black communities, a substantial proportion of minority voters must be concentrated in a district to ensure that minorities can outvote whites. Edward Still (1992) noted that districts drawn with a 65 percent African American population are perhaps the bare minimum required to facilitate African American representation, although Brace et al. (1988) noted that this minimum varies greatly by place. Lublin (1997) suggested that it can go below 55 percent in many parts of the country (see also Grofman and Handley 1989).

Regardless of the threshold, the practice of majority-minority districting creates a set of political and normative problems, if not trade-offs, for a democracy. Concentration of minority vote strength in districts for the purpose of descriptive representation can produce less "substantive" representation of minority concerns. This results from the loss of "influence" that minority voters would have had over white representatives they could have helped to elect were they not concentrated in majority-minority districts (Swain 1993; Lublin 1997). "Packing" minority votes into majority-minority districts may thus "waste" minority votes (Still 1984). Others suggest that this form of districting can limit minority influence over policy (Guinier 1991; 1998; Sass and Mehay n.d.) and prevent the formation of coalitions across racial lines (Swain 1993). Majority-minority districting solutions are facing an increasing number of practical, political, and legal challenges. Since majority-minority districts will almost inevitably be safe seats for one party, their use can quite possibly lead to less competitive elections, which might depress turnout.[8] And, as Lani Guinier noted, majority-minority districts may create legislative settings where most representatives have no need to appeal to minority voters or work with minority representatives (1991; 1998).

Whatever the appeal of these critiques, the courts have added to the barriers against majority-minority districts created in the *Miller, Shaw,* and *Hunt* decisions. Through much of the 1980s and 1990s, preclearence meant that state and local jurisdictions had the burden of proving that any change in election rules (including drawing new district maps) did not have the purpose and effect of denying opportunities for representation on account of race or color. In 2000, however, a narrow 5-4 majority retreated from precedent and practice in ruling that the Justice Department had to approve new election rules having a "discriminatory purpose" as long as the new rules left minority voters in no worse a position than before (*Reno v. Bossier Parish School Board* 2000).[9] In the Bossier Parish challenge to a twelve-district election plan, a plurality of the court reasoned that blacks had previously been elected without a majority black district, so they could not be made worse off by a plan lacking such districts. Future use of the VRA to increase minority representation via majority-minority districting will be more difficult than in the past two decades.

A Brief History of Cumulative and Limited Voting Elections

Although cumulative voting (CV) has not been used in national-level elections and use of limited voting (LV) has been quite rare, U.S. experiments with CV and LV at the local level are not unique. Even within the United States, CV has long been used in elections for the governing bodies of corporations and was used to elect the Illinois State House for much of the twentieth century (Blair 1958; Sawyer and MacRae 1962; Goldburg 1994). Previous use of CV and LV not only predates these examples but also was motivated by issues of minority representation. The first example of CV actually used in practice came in Victorian times in elections to the Cape Legislative Council (1854 to 1890), the upper house of the Cape Colony's (South Africa) legislature. The main justification was that it protected minority rights. The *Report from a Committee of the Board of Trade and Plantations* (January 30, 1850) justified the system on the following grounds:

> By this arrangement, a monopoly of power in the Legislative Council by any one party, or any one district of the Colony, would be prevented, since a minority of the electors, by giving all their votes to a single candidate, would be enabled to secure his return. (quoted in Grey 1853, 363)[10]

This is an unambiguous statement of the relevance of CV for minority representation and resonates strongly with current debates over the adoption of this system in the United States (Guinier 1991).[11] The fact that English settlers were the relevant minority in Cape Colony helps to explain London's concern for minority rights. London worried that the English would be overwhelmed by the more numerous Boers in majoritarian elections and designed an election system to give the English opportunities for representation. At the same time, discussions over property qualifications of voters saw London policy makers pushing a relatively low property qualification. This resulted in extending the franchise to nonwhite voters, who were more likely to side with the English than the Boers (Trapido 1964).[12]

In England CV was used in school board elections from 1870 to 1902, when elections were contested over the issue of religious instruction in schools. Fierce debates raged over the extent to which religious instruction should be allowed and, within the religious bloc, whether and how Catholicism should be included in the curriculum (see Sutherland 1973 for an overview). CV was adopted for these elections in order to give a platform to competing minority views on the subject. Later these elections were the battleground for a variety of secular social movements and especially the Labour and Suffragist movements (McCann 1960).[13]

McMillan (1997) provides an excellent historical account of the introduction and use of the limited vote in U.K. parliamentary elections as a result of the Second Reform Act of 1867 "largely as a result of pressure to reduce the impact of the extension of the franchise included in the measure" (85). In this case, extension of the franchise worried those who feared being reduced to weak minority status once a larger pool of citizens would be voting. Outcomes under LV are expected to be more proportionate the more limited the vote is relative to the number of seats at stake (for a description, see Lakeman 1974, 80–88; Still 1984, 253–55).

Illinois adopted CV in the same era in response to the need to protect minority representation. As Dunn (1972) illustrated, CV was employed to solve a practical political problem. After the U.S. Civil War, support for Illinois parties was sharply divided along regional lines. Democrats dominated in the south of the state and Republicans in the north, so winner-take-all SMSP districts made it nearly impossible for a Democrat to win in the north or a Republican in the south. Dunn noted that CV accomplished its goal of providing minority party representation in each region, but that it provided little minor party representation. Only a few third-party candidates were elected under CV in Illinois (Dunn 1972, 634). The U.S. House of Representatives also considered CV in 1869, 1870, and 1871 in response to votes-seats distortions that were exacerbated by sectional voting.

In sum, the systems of CV and LV have been introduced to help bring about a more proportional reflection of underlying social cleavages in elected bodies. Indeed, CV and LV are often categorized as "semiproportionate" in classifications of electoral systems, since they can "waste" more votes than fully proportional systems (Amy 1993; Lakeman 1974). Unlike STV or party list PR, CV and LV allow a winning candidate to collect more votes than the minimum quota required to win a seat. However, compared to majoritarian rules, CV and LV allow candidates to win with much less than a plurality. While these examples point to the potential for gains in minority representation using these alternative systems, there is also room for some caution. There are reasons to expect some deviations from proportional (descriptive) representation in CV and LV places, and these reasons are tied to the capacity of voters and elites to engage in strategic behavior.

The Rise of Cumulative and Limited Voting in the United States

Away from the fury over majority-minority districting, a small number of U.S. localities began new experiments with election rules that departed from the nation's majoritarian/plurality traditions. Several scholars have advocated CV and LV in response to the perceived limits of districting (see in particular Guinier

1997; "Alternative Voting Systems" 1982; Still 1984). In the late 1980s, Alamogordo, New Mexico, and Chilton County, Alabama, began contesting elections under CV in response to VRA actions brought by minority plaintiffs.

At issue in Alamogordo was the inability of Latinos to win seats on the city's seven-member council. In 1983, Alamogordo adopted a "mixed" election system that had four SMDs and three at-large seats. Latinos made up over 21 percent of the city's voting-age population (the city was also 5 percent black), yet no minority had been elected at large since 1970 (Engstrom, Taebel, and Cole 1989). No Hispanic and black plaintiffs filed suit against the at-large plan in 1986. Drawing majority-minority districts was possible in Alamogordo but was complicated by the dispersion of Latinos and by the fact that many minority residents were military personnel who rarely voted in city elections (Engstrom, Taebel, and Cole 1989, 482). CV was found acceptable to both minority plaintiffs and defendants and was ordered as a remedy to vote dilution by a judge (Taebel, Engstrom, and Cole 1988, 26). In the city's first CV election in 1987, Inez Moncada finished third in an eight-candidate field, winning one of the three at-large seats elected by CV. She was the first Hispanic elected since 1968.

In Chilton County, Alabama, 10 percent of the county's voting-age residents were black, yet no black had been elected to the county commission since Reconstruction. A private attorney suggested CV, which was accepted in part because "the leading statewide black political organization" endorsed alternative electoral systems such as LV and CV early on (Pildes and Donoghue 1995, 266). In the first CV election in Chilton County, Bobby Agee led a fourteen-candidate field with the most votes, becoming the first African American county commissioner since Reconstruction (Pildes and Donoghue 1995, 272).

By the 1990s, dozens of additional jurisdictions in Texas and Alabama responded to VRA action by adopting CV, while a number of places in Alabama and North Carolina began using LV. In 1995, Pildes and Donoghue reported (1995, 266) that at least twenty small jurisdictions in Alabama were using LV, in part due to support for the plan from a state organization advocating representation of blacks. Between 1991 and 1995 at least two dozen small cities and school districts in the Texas Panhandle and Permian Basin areas settled VRA suits by adopting CV. The League of United Latin American Citizens (LULAC) (Brischetto 1995, 6) filed nearly all of these suits. Table 2.1 lists some of the local jurisdictions in the United States that have adopted CV and LV election plans. Although there is no single entity monitoring use of CV or LV plans, our research has identified about 100 towns, cities, counties, and school districts that use these alternative elections (see Appendix A).

Typically these are small, rural, and southern communities that previously elected their representatives under standard at-large plurality rules that restricted the ability of minority groups to win seats. Studies of elections held under CV

TABLE 2.1. Partial List of Jurisdictions Adopting CV and LV in the United States

Place	Body Elected	Year Adopted	CV or LV
Alomagordo, New Mexico	City Council	1987	CV
Webb, Alabama	City Council	1987	LV
Centre, Alabama	City Council	1988	LV
Chilton County, Alabama	County Commission	1988	CV
Chilton County, Alabama	Dem. Party Com.	1988	CV
Guin, Alabama	City Council	1988	CV
Sisseton, South Dakota	School Board	1989	CV
Lockhart, Texas	School Board	1991	CV
Peoria, Illinois	City Council	1991	CV
Dora, Alabama	City Council	1992	LV
Yorktown, Texas	School Board	1992	CV
Yoakum, Texas	School Board	1993	CV
Anson, Texas	City Council	1994	CV
Beaufort County, North Carolina	County Commission	1994	LV
Bladen County, North Carolina	County Commission	1994	LV
Denver City, Texas	School Board	1994	CV
Andrews, Texas	School Board	1994	CV
Friona, Texas	City Council	1994	CV
Grapeland, Texas	City Council	1994	LV
Anson County, North Carolina	School Board	1995	LV
Anton, Texas	City Council	1996	CV
O'Donnel, Texas	City Council	1996	CV
Bourne, Texas	City Council	1997	CV
Jourdonton, Texas	City Council	1997	CV
Hamlin, Texas	School Board	1998	CV
Amarillo, Texas	School Board	2000	CV

have documented that these systems have helped Native Americans (Engstrom and Barrilleaux 1991), African Americans (Brischetto 1995), and Latinos (Brischetto and Engstrom 1997) win seats in places where they have rarely, if ever, been successful (also Pildes and Donoghue 1995; Cole and Taebel 1992; Cole, Taebel, and Engstrom 1990).[14]

In some places, CV was adopted as a compromise between plaintiffs seeking districts and defendants (governments) hostile to that idea. At other times it was adopted to save the time and cost of drawing districts. In Alabama, Texas, and North Carolina, much of the credit for the diffusion of CV and LV plans as solutions to VRA suits can be given to a handful of attorneys who advocated the plans on behalf of minority plaintiffs. If more attorneys were ready to propose these solutions, it is highly likely that they would be used more frequently.[15] Some CV advocates suggest that these elections, in addition to their cost-saving appeal and their ability to facilitate minority representation, could produce qualitative changes beneficial to democratic practices. There are numerous suggestions along on these lines. It is said that by avoiding the acrimonious process of districting, CV might diffuse racial tensions and might also grant minorities more clout in legislative bodies (Sass and Mehay n.d.; Guiner 1994). It is also suggested that by avoiding "safe seat" districts, politics can be more dynamic in CV places because coalitions may be rebuilt after each election, as candidates have the flexibility to appeal to new groups of voters through an entire jurisdiction rather than a single district ("Alternative Voting Systems" 1982).

How Cumulative and Limited Voting Elections Work in the United States

CV systems have multimember districts where voters are given as many votes as there are seats (e.g., they are given four votes in a four-seat district, five in a five-seat district, and so on). Voters are allowed to distribute votes among the candidates however they see fit. In a five-seat district, for example, a voter could give all five votes to one candidate, give one each to five separate candidates, or give three votes to candidate A and one each to candidate B and candidate C. In fact, any combination of integers that added up to five would be permissible.[16] An example of a CV ballot from Guin, Alabama, is provided in figure 2.1. Although most implementations of CV allow voters to distribute their votes as they choose, at least one (Peoria, Illinois) constrains how votes are cast by providing only one space next to each candidate (then dividing five votes equally across the number of candidates marked). In this, Peoria follows traditional Illinois code.

Under LV, voters are allowed fewer votes than there are seats available. Even when LV allows voters to cast multiple votes, they can give only one vote to any candidate. As we will see, the net effect of CV and LV is to lower the proportion of votes that a candidate needs to win a seat. In these elections, unlike SMD elections and standard at-large elections, candidates who receive less than a plurality may nevertheless win seats.

Table 2.2 illustrates some important points about variation across modified at-large election plans in U.S. places having 1,000 or more population. These data reflect information about elections from jurisdictions that will be used in our estimation of turnout and representation under CV. Clearly, there is no single CV or LV plan. Most places using CV elect their entire council at large with CV—although a small number of places mix CV with SMDs (an example being Alamagordo, New Mexico). Across all CV places, the average number of seats elected is only slightly lower than the average number of total seats (6.30 vs. 6.44). Table 2.2 shows that these elections tend to occur in places having significant minority populations.

Table 2.2 also demonstrates that many CV places do not elect all seats in a single election. In places outside of Texas, the entire board or council (typically five to seven members) is typically elected in a single election with CV. Yet in Texas, although the entire council is often elected by CV, elections are staggered over time such that only two or three seats are elected at any one time in a single contest. This causes the average number of seats elected via CV per place per election cycle (3.13) to be substantially less than the average number of total seats per place (6.44).

In about one-third of places using LV, some seats are elected from SMDs, with the remainder elected from multimember districts at large. Conversely, about two-thirds of the places using LV elect all council seats from at-large, multimember districts. Few of these places elect all seats in the same election (most stagger elections). For this reason, places often limit voters to two votes,

FIGURE 2.1. Sample CV Ballot

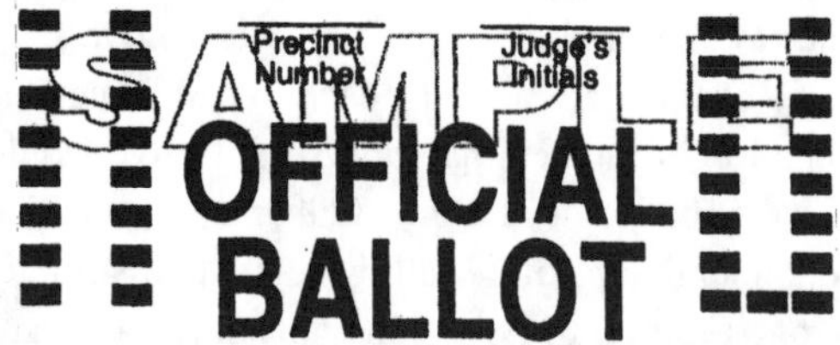

INSTRUCTIONS TO VOTERS

TO VOTE, COMPLETE THE ARROW POINTING TO YOUR CHOICE, LIKE THIS: ▶━━▶. Mark With BLACK Felt Tip Pen (NO RED INK). To cast a write-in vote, complete the arrow to the left of the blank line provided and write the candidate's name in that space. For specific write-in instructions, refer to the card of instructions located in the booth.

If you tear, soil, deface or erroneously mark this ballot, return it to the election judge and obtain another.

INSTRUCTIONS TO VOTERS

The maximum number of votes you may cast for City Councilman-At-Large is FIVE (5).

-If you vote for one (1) candidate, the candidate receives 5 votes.

-If you vote for two (2) candidates, each candidate receives 2 1/2 votes.

-If you vote for three (3) candidates, each candidate receives 1 2/3 votes.

-If you vote for four (4) candidates, each candidate receives 1 1/4 votes.

-If you vote for five (5) candidates, each candidate receives 1 vote.

COUNCILMAN-AT-LARGE
FOR CITY COUNCILMAN-AT-LARGE (Vote For One, Two, Three, Four, or Five)
JIM ARDIS III
W. ERIC TURNER
SIE MAROON
JOHN MORRIS
CHARLES V. GRAYEB
BILL O'BRIEN
JERRY LISENBY
CARTHEDA WELCH
BETTY D. JONES
LEONARD A. UNES
GARY V. SANDBERG
WRITE-IN
WRITE-IN
WRITE-IN
WRITE-IN
WRITE-IN

TABLE 2.2. Cumulative and Limited Voting Arrangements in U.S. Communities

Cumulative Voting:	
Number of elections	94
Average number of total council seats per place	6.44
Average number elected at large with CV per place	6.30
Average number elected with CV per elections[a]	3.13
Average number of minority seats per place[b]	0.56
Average population	7,948
Average percent voting-age population minority[b]	31
Limited Voting:	
Number of cases (elections)	17
Average number of total council seats per place	7.06
Average number elected at large with LV per place	4.94
Average number elected with LV per election	4.00
Average number of minority seats per place[b]	1.06
Modal vote limit	1
Average population	19,363
Average percent voting-age population minority[b]	30

Note: Cases used for averages are based on individual elections.

[a] "Per election" reflects average number of seats on a council at stake per election. Some places elect part of the council in different years; others elect all seats at once.
[b] Figures are for the largest minority group only.

typically cast in an election with three or four seats up (average. = 4.00). LV plans include further variation. At least one county uses place requirements (a candidate must reside in a specific multimember district elected via LV) and uses more than one multimember district. A small number of places allow voters to cast two to four votes, depending on how many seats are elected.

The reason why CV may help benefit minorities is that minorities can pool their votes in order to ensure their representation. There are a variety of ways we can represent this. One standard way of discussing it is by reference to the *threshold of representation,* which is the minimum support necessary to earn a party (or candidate) representation. This value reflects the level of support that would earn a seat in the unlikely event that all candidates earned nearly the same vote totals. An alternative measure is the *threshold of exclusion,* which is the maximum support that can be attained by a party or candidate that nevertheless fails to gain representation. The threshold of representation provides a necessary condition for representation, while the threshold of exclusion provides a sufficient condition (Grofman 1975, 311).[17] The latter value is important for those concerned about minority representation, as it reflects the level of support that a

TABLE 2.3. Thresholds of Representation and Exclusion under Plurality, CV, LV, D'Hondt, and Largest Remainder

Formula	Plurality	Limited Voting	Cumulative Voting	D'Hondt	Largest Remainder
Threshold of Exclusion	1/2	k/(k + m)	1/m + 1	1/m + 1	1/2 m
Threshold of Representation	1/n	min [1/n, k/(k + m + n − 2)]	1/(mn − m + 1)	1/m + n − 1	1/mn

Note: m = number of members being elected from a given district, *n* = number of parties contesting the election, *k* = number of votes cast. In the LV example, the vote is limited to one.
Source: Grofman (1975, 313); Rae, Hanby, and Loosemore (1971).

candidate can receive yet still win no seat. Put differently, if a minority group voted as a perfectly cohesive block and directed all votes to a single candidate, the threshold of exclusion would represent the maximum vote share the candidate could receive while still being denied a seat.

The formulas used to calculate these values are expressed in table 2.3. This provides a means of comparing the barriers to minority representation associated with standard plurality at-large elections and with LV and CV elections. The lower part of table 2.3 illustrates what the actual values of these threshold would be when eight candidates contested an election for four seats in a multimember district (or four at-large seats). From the formulas for threshold of exclusion we can see that in general LV and CV have much lower thresholds of exclusion than do simple-plurality systems. At worst, CV and LV should produce the same outcome as plurality; at best it is possible to obtain proportionality of representation. In the example used in the table, a candidate receiving just over 20 percent support would be elected.

Although the broad outlines of CV and LV systems are similar across U.S. jurisdictions that have adopted them, some differences in implementation of these alternative plans do exist, and these differences can have important consequences for what the threshold of exclusion might be in any particular place. Differences in CV and LV thresholds under various election plans can be affected by two main factors: the rules regarding vote allocations and the number of seats elected via CV or LV. Election rules determine the number of seats elected under CV or LV directly, by reducing or enlarging the number of seats in a given jurisdiction, or indirectly, through staggering the elections of those seats across time. Figure 2.2 illustrates how variation in the number of seats affects the threshold of exclusion in a jurisdiction. As the number of seats to be elected shrinks, the size of the vote share needed to ensure a representative increases.

FIGURE 2.2. Threshold of Exclusion by Number of Seats Contested under CV

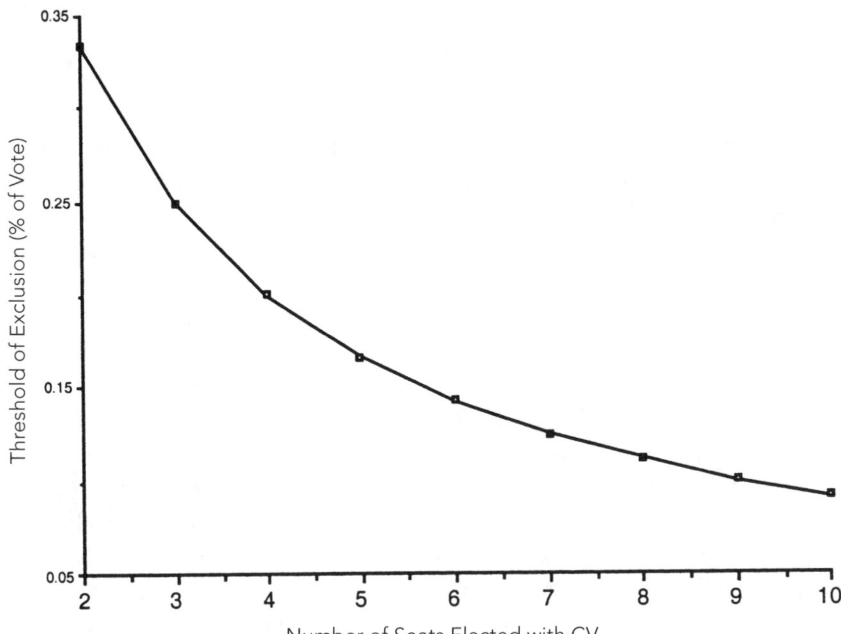

Take, for example, the threshold of exclusion for CV. With only two seats, minorities need to have 1/(2 + 1) or one-third of the population to ensure representation: with five seats, minorities require 1/(5 + 1) or one-sixth. By manipulating the number of seats, local officials can thus make it easier (or harder) for minorities to gain representation.

Figure 2.2 should be interpreted with some caution. It might be tempting, for example, to expect that a four-seat CV election will produce representation for a minority community that has something just over a 20 percent share of a jurisdiction's population. Yet we cannot assume that support for a minority candidate will reach the threshold of exclusion, even if a highly cohesive minority group votes in the election. If minority votes end up divided across two or more candidates, no single candidate will exceed the threshold. Even if a single minority candidate is nominated, low turnout among minority voters could prevent a single candidate from reaching the threshold. Although the literature on the mechanics on these systems dates back to John Stuart Mill, U.S. Senator Buckalew in 1872, Dodgson (Lewis Carroll) in 1884, and Gerstenberg in 1910, it is worth discussing in some detail the effects these systems are likely to produce for voters, parties, and candidates (Buckalew 1872; Dodgson 1884). We turn our attention to this in the next chapter.

As systems allowing voters to cast various combinations of votes, LV and CV in particular require a certain level of coordination between voters and candidates (or parties) if minority candidates are to win or if results are to approach proportionality. Minority representation under CV and LV depends in large part upon voters' acting strategically in how they distribute their multiple votes, and it requires that minority voters turn out and participate at levels similar to whites. Some form of political organization may have to communicate information about vote strategies for this to occur. Mobilization efforts may also be required. As we shall see, there may be a need to control the nomination of candidates.

This means that the prospects for minority representation are very different under CV and LV than under SMD plans drawn with majority-minority districts. Whereas district cartography can very often ensure that a minority candidate will be elected to a particular seat, CV and LV plans cannot provide the same kind of certainty. There is no "automatic" mechanical effect to ensure, for example, that an election plan with a 20 percent threshold of exclusion will provide a minority representative in a jurisdiction that is 20, 30, or 40 percent black or Latino. It is not surprising, then, that one primary concern of minority advocates is that minority communities could end up underrepresented in these "alternative systems" due to the strategic demands the rules place on voters, candidates, and political organizations.

A Comparison between Cumulative Voting and Systems of Proportional Representation

CV is one of a family of ordinal electoral systems that includes STV and the alternative vote (AV), the latter sometimes known as the instant runoff. These ordinal systems tend to be less studied than other kinds of electoral systems—such as "list" PR—that aim to produce "fairer" outcomes (Bowler 1996; Bowler and Grofman 2000). Ordinal systems such as CV are unique when compared to other election systems, since they allow for a rather fluid accounting of voter preferences (as do some PR systems), while retaining the candidate-centered (as opposed to party-centered) style of representation that usually characterizes SMSP district elections.

There are important differences between purely proportional systems such as list PR and ordinal systems such as STV and CV that hinge on the structure of the ballot. Like the SMSP system, most PR systems (such as those used in the Netherlands and South Africa) allow voters to express a preference for one, and only one, party or candidate. This is sometimes known as categorical voting (Rae 1971; Farrell 2001) and allows voters to express a choice for their most preferred candidate or party.

Under PR systems the choice allowed is typically over party rather than candidate and reflects a very different conception of representation from that underpinning SMDs. SMD systems reflect the idea that voters would like to vote for individual candidates who would then go on to represent the interests of a geographic area. Under list-PR systems, the personalities and qualities of individual candidates are decidedly secondary to the party and party label. Voters are given a choice of parties, with the share of seats in a legislature given to the party in proportion to the share of the vote each party receives over some very large multimember district. Typically, the larger the district and hence the larger the number of seats to be won (district magnitude), the easier it is to allocate seats proportionally. It is easier to allocate 100 seats proportionally among six or seven parties than it is to allocate five. The individual politicians who take up seats in the legislature are in the hands of the party organization that maintains lists of candidates (hence the term *list PR*).[18] Furthermore, the idea of representing a geographic area is secondary to the idea that social groups may need representation, as in South Africa with the case of ethnic groups or in the Netherlands with the case of social and religious groups. As we have noted, this property of PR has led some reformers to advocate its adoption in the United States as a remedy for minority underrepresentation (Amy 1993; Barber 2000).

Both the districted (SMSP) system and list PR have their share of critics. We have discussed the failings of the first of these in terms of the results it produces. Results under SMSP are usually not proportional to the outcome, especially for smaller parties (e.g., for Britain's Liberal Democrats). While proportional systems may be fairer, for some analysts they may be too fair. PR is often criticized because it may produce multipartyism that sometimes leads to chaotic government—the limiting cases here being those of Italy, Israel, France's Fourth Republic, and Weimar Germany. List PR is, moreover, often held to break the link between individual representative and the voter, since typically the voter is not allowed to cast a ballot for an individual candidate.[19]

By contrast, ordinal systems typically allow voters to express multiple preferences or to rank-order their preferences. The preferential systems of STV and AV allow voters to express an explicit preference ranking of whom they like most, whom they like second best, and so on. Under CV, voters are implicitly allowed this option by being allowed to give more votes to a preferred candidate. This ordering of preferences is simply not permissible under categorical ballots. It gives voters the freedom to combine or shade preferences in the manner of their choice. Under STV, for example, even though a voter may be fairly loyal to a particular party, he or she can rank an appealing candidate from a rival party higher than someone from his or her "own" party. Under CV a rough equivalent is that the voter could give a few votes to that appealing candidate.

Loosely speaking, ordinal systems occupy a middle ground between list PR

FIGURE 2.3. Ballot Structure and Electoral Systems

		Extent of Choice	
		Categorical Voting	**Ordinal Voting**
Nature of Choice	Candidate based	Single member simple plurality (E.g., U.K., India, Canada)	Cumulative vote, single transferable vote (STV), alternative vote (E.g., Australia, Ireland, Malta)
	Party based	Closed-list PR (E.g., Netherlands, Sweden, South Africa)	Open-list PR (E.g., Finland)

Source: Farrell (2001, 170).

and SMSP by allowing voters to express a preference for individual candidates and aiming for a rough proportionality of outcome. Figure 2.3 places ordinal electoral systems in a comparative framework according to how many choices voters are allowed and how those choices are structured. We can distinguish between ballots that allow voters to express just their first preference (categorical voting) and those that allow voters to express several preferences (ordinal voting). We can also distinguish between those ballots that allow voting for individual candidates and those that structure choice along party lines (Rae 1971; Bowler and Farrell 1993; Farrell 2001).

Ordinal systems thus attempt to combine different features of electoral systems by allowing voters to cast a ballot for specific candidates within districts while also producing a more "fair" result than might result if SMSP districts were used.[20] The major difference between ordinal systems and the more familiar list-PR systems is that while the latter *will* (by definition) produce proportional outcomes, ordinal systems *might* do this, but only under certain conditions. Under ordinal systems such as CV, the outcome, as we show throughout this book, depends substantially on what voters and candidates do. For this reason, analysts describe systems such as CV as "rough" methods of PR (Blair 1958, 123). We should also note that since results from ordinal systems are heavily contingent on how candidates and voters respond to the election system, these systems provide for a much richer range of feasible outcomes than either SMSP or list PR.

STV, in contrast to CV or LV, is probably more reliable in producing minority representation, since vote coordination and nomination problems are sorted out, in part, when ranked preferences for candidates are transferred as votes are counted (Ritchie and Hill 1999). But CV and LV, while still rare, are the systems that have emerged more commonly on the U.S. landscape as practical alternatives to districting. In the next chapter, we begin assessing the demands these systems place on voters and candidates. In subsequent chapters, we examine how groups, candidates, and voters respond to the demands created by these new election rules.

· 3 ·

The Strategic Demands of Cumulative and Limited Voting

Coordination Problems Facing Voters

Much of the potential for modified at-large plans such as cumulative and limited voting (CV and LV) to produce deviations from proportionality lies in the demands for strategic coordination that each system places at the mass and elite levels (Cox 1997). Under each system, both candidates and voters must engage in some fairly sophisticated strategic thinking and behavior. Formal analyses of what CV *could* produce in terms of proportionate outcomes make a number of assumptions, most notably that voters distribute their votes equally among candidates (for discussion, see Gerber, Morton, and Rietz 1998). As we will see below, this is a far from innocuous assumption to make when these systems are implemented, even though it adds to analytic tractability. Under CV, voters have to decide not only for whom to vote but also *how* to vote for them (i.e., whether and how to cumulate their votes).

The problems this poses for voters can be simply illustrated in table 3.1. Here, by construction, two candidates from a party could win two seats in a five-seat district provided two of its candidates receive five votes. Consider this as a simplified example of a case where voters must coordinate their behavior in order to maximize how many of their desired candidates are elected. Assume that two voters would like each of the party's candidates to get elected. A voter may cast anywhere from zero to five votes and may give any combination to candidate 1 (c1) and or candidate 2 (c2). Table 3.1 illustrates the possible ways a voter could distribute votes across two candidates, and cell entries reflect the resulting votes for c1, followed by votes for c2. The instances where the voters combine their votes such that both candidates meet the five-vote threshold can be seen in the table along the darkly shaded diagonal.

The vote coordination problem can be seen in the fact that most combinations of votes would result in the election of only one of the preferred candidates. Vot-

TABLE 3.1. Possible Vote Distributions for Two Voters and Their Consequences for the Vote Shares of Two Candidates (c1 and c2) under CV

		Voter B					
	Votes	**5,0**	**4,1**	**3,2**	**2,3**	**1,4**	**0,5**
	5,0	10,0	9,1	8,2	7,3	6,4	5,5
Voter	**4,1**	9,1	8,2	7,3	6,4	5,5	4,6
A	**3,2**	8,2	7,3	6,4	5,5	4,6	3,7
	2,3	7,3	6,4	5,5	4,6	3,7	2,8
	1,4	6,4	5,5	4,6	3,7	2,8	1,9
	0,5	5,5	4,6	3,7	2,8	1,9	0,10

Note: Numbers in boldface along the margins refer to the distribution of votes case for candidate 1 (c1) and candidate 2 (c2), respectively. Cell entries are total vote shares for c1 and c2, respectively.

ers must, therefore, somehow agree to fill in their ballot such that when voter A gives one candidate (c1) three votes and the other (c2) two, voter B knows to give c1 two votes and c2 three in order to make sure that both candidates have exactly five votes. If they do not coordinate their votes in one of these ways, only one candidate will win.

The table can also represent another situation with a related problem of coordination. Assume that conditions remain the same, except that now the threshold for election is ten votes. The party still has two candidates seeking seats. If only one of the candidates may win and requires ten votes to do so, then the voters need to "plump"—that is, they must cast all their votes for one candidate. In this situation the voters must somehow agree among themselves which candidate to make a winner. The two lightly shaded boxes in the corners of table 3.1 represent this situation. Here, if voters fail to agree on which candidate to back, it is very possible to see *both* of them lose. In either case it is not clear how voters left to their own devices can easily overcome these coordination problems in large electorates.

The problems evident in table 3.1 reflect, in a simple form, the difficulties that any group faces when contesting CV and LV elections. Moreover, as the number of voters increases, the number of seats up for grabs (district magnitude) mounts, and the number of candidates per seat increases, these problems become both more urgent and also more difficult to solve. Little wonder, then, at Rae's (1971) comment on systems of this kind: "One would expect that the rather complex cognitive arrangements necessary for ordinal voting are likely to be quite rare" (128).[1] This brings us to some questions we will answer later on: How well do real-world candidates and voters deal with these problems? And how do their attempts to deal with the problems affect democratic practices?

We should note at this point that, in some cases, the coordination problem may not be posed so sharply. For example, where candidates from the same party do not need an exactly equal vote share to maximize the seats they win, voters have room to make more mistakes. Likewise, in situations where just one candidate from a minority group is running, voters may find it relatively straightforward to plump. But the broader lesson illustrated by these examples is that in some situations voters have to behave in a very particular way (split their vote, plump their vote) to maximize the number of candidates they elect relative to their electoral strength. Moreover, voters must not only coordinate their behaviors but also recognize which situation they are in.

This issue of voters' abilities to coordinate the way they cast their ballots received some attention in previous studies of the use of CV in Illinois state legislative elections. The Illinois case is probably one of the best studied applications of CV, although because it is a partisan election context, it is not perfectly analogous to most of the CV and LV elections at the local level in the United States. For decades, the Illinois legislature was elected by CV from three-member districts. Electoral politics in Illinois illustrates ways that candidates and parties responded to the coordination demands created by CV. The development of electoral cartels between Democratic and Republican party officials, for example, led to deals being cut about how many candidates each party would nominate across the state.[2] These deals typically limited the total number of candidates in any district to three, with the stronger party in a district given the prerogative of nominating two candidates (Sawyer and MacRae 1962; Reapportionment Hearings 1965, 64). Low district magnitude, state party control of nominations, and reasonably strong party loyalties on the part of voters thus eliminated much need to worry about how voters cast their ballots. Electoral rules further eased demands for vote coordination in important ways by effectively allowing party-list voting with one mark of the ballot. As Silva (1964) noted, "When a party runs three candidates a cross in the party box is counted as one vote for each. With two candidates such a cross is counted as 1 vote for each; with one, three votes for that candidate" (754, n. 36).

Through the electoral code, then, Illinois parties were able to accomplish vote management and equal vote share. These are vitally important achievements. Given both party collusion and the ticket vote, it is of little surprise that subsequent analyses found Illinois elections to exhibit straight-party voting and strategic undernomination of candidates in districts (Sawyer and MacRae 1962; Goldburg 1994). This means, furthermore, that the experience of CV in Illinois legislative elections is not the best guide to the workings of CV under conditions lacking parties, having more than two parties, having greater district magnitude, or featuring combinations of these factors. It also suggests a limit to the usefulness of approaches that assume that elections across districts involve only decisions within the districts (Goldburg 1994). This can ignore what may be termed the "real" (cartel) game that operated in Illinois. As we shall see below, CV elsewhere has involved both more seats per district and more parties, making for a more complex choice setting both for voters and for party managers. In these settings it becomes much harder for parties to solve voters' coordination problems by making nomination trades across districts.

LV presents, in general, a somewhat easier task for voters, particularly if the vote is limited to one. In restricting voters to casting only one vote per candidate, LV imposes a de facto equal distribution of votes and so removes a layer of coordination problems entirely. The strategic problem facing voters under LV, then, is presented when overnomination occurs and voters have multiple votes to cast. As a result, Still (1984, 256) suggested that CV is likely to place greater strategic burdens on voter than LV (on the possibility of strategic mistakes by minority voters in CV, also see Aspin and Hall 1996 and Engstrom 1993).

Since CV allows voters more options when delivering their votes, the existence of such opportunities increases the probability that some minority voters will spread votes across multiple candidates, even if only one minority candidate is running. This in turn, increases the chance that minority votes may go to nonminority candidates, thereby limiting the translation of minority vote strength into seats. Furthermore, in CV or LV places where a group's population share is near the threshold of exclusion and voting is racially polarized, minority candidates can be elected only if their supporters turn out at a rate matching majority-group voters. The weight of these demands suggests that descriptive representation of minorities under CV and LV might easily be less proportionate to population than that obtained by election systems that concentrate minorities in single-member districts. Only some level of organizational activity will help solve problems but, as we see in the following section, parties and candidates must solve their own coordination problems before helping voters to solve theirs.

Coordination Problems Facing Parties and Candidates

The coordination problems facing voters are matched by similar problems facing parties or political groups contesting nonpartisan elections. A group can (potentially) maximize seats by controlling the candidate selection process such that it places an optimal number of candidates on the ballot. To do this, the group must know how many candidates to nominate given its expected vote share and its "opponent's" nomination plans (Goldburg 1994, 886; Brams 1975; Silva 1964; Sawyer and McRae 1962). If a group overnominates and too many candidates are listed, the group risks spreading the votes of supporters too thin, thereby risking underrepresentation. If a group undernominates, it errs by wasting votes that might have yielded another seat. In the four-seat example above, a group controlling 20 percent of votes would optimally nominate only one candidate.

Thus a party or slating group must effectively maximize seats by controlling the candidate selection process such that they place an optimal number of candidates on the ballot. With multiple candidates, voters of a group near the threshold of exclusion must know which candidate to plump for if they are to win a seat. If they are in a position to secure multiple seats, the group must also know how to spread their supporters' votes accurately across candidates (Still 1984, 254–55).[3] Victorian politicians expressly recognized these problems of overnomination very early on (Bowler, Donovan, and Farrell 1999).[4] In the appendix to this chapter, we include a more formal description of potential nomination problems under CV.

Plainly, electoral outcomes under CV depend upon the interaction between voters and parties and are contingent upon the ability of parties, candidates, and voters to act strategically. In particular, they are contingent on the fact that voters and candidates *must* act strategically if a group is to obtain representation. These strategic concerns raise some questions for the applicability of CV as a remedy for minority underrepresentation. While in principle these strategic burdens apply to large and small groups alike (Goldburg 1994; Silva 1964), in practice the burdens may be felt quite unequally.

We might plausibly expect, for example, that minority groups are likely to be poorer, less well organized, and generally less experienced than those in the majority. In a practical sense, then, strategic burdens may be greater for minority groups. By contrast, others argue that strategic burdens may be felt most strongly among bigger groups and specifically among the majority rather than the minority. Lijphart (1994) and others suggest that LV (Single Non-Transferable Vote [SNTV]) systems might be legitimately considered as PR, since the strategic burdens are often likely to be greater for majorities than for minorities. A minority group often need to nominate only one candidate to ensure some representation. Majority groups, by contrast, may run a greater risk of nomination errors (Lijphart 1994, 42; Taagepera and Shugart 1989; see also Cox 1991).

With majority-minority districts, however, group representation can be achieved largely via district cartography rather than mobilization efforts or the activities of individual candidates and so may offer a somewhat surer, but less flexible path, to minority representation.

Similar Outcomes Do Not Mean Similar Processes

By way of concluding this chapter, and by way of preface to the empirical material that follows, we can make some more general remarks about electoral institutions. The discussion of how ordinal systems in general, and CV and LV in particular, depend upon the capacity of voters and candidates to behave strategically illustrates a number of points that lead us to be a bit cautious in our assessment about the likely impact of changes in electoral institutions on descriptive representation.[5]

The tone of the literature to date is one of an enthusiastic band of electoral engineers who are keen to juggle electoral laws to produce some desired representation outcome. While this is more true of the literature by those interested in reforming electoral régimes than of the academic literature, there is sometimes an assumption of precision about electoral engineering in the comparative literature too. There are, however, reasons to be skeptical that changing electoral systems will produce changes in patterns of representation.

First, the discussion of coordination problems under CV/LV shows that if the strategizing of minorities fails while the majority mobilizes successfully, then these new electoral arrangements may produce outcomes that could, conceivably, be even worse for minorities than what might be obtained with districting. Alternatively, if minorities are good at behaving strategically while the majority is bad at it, then minorities can gain more than proportional representation.[6]

Appendix

Nomination Problems under CV

Table 3.2 presents a matrix that illustrates optimal nomination strategies given various levels of vote shares, across different numbers of seats being contested under CV, but the logic can be extended to LV systems that produce similar thresholds of exclusion. Optimal nominations are defined as

$$Vs/T, \text{ rounded to lowest near whole integer, where } T = (1/(1 + n)) * 100$$

where Vs is vote share, n is the number of seats contested, and T is the threshold of exclusion as listed for each electoral arrangement at the bottom of the table. The display in this table is based on the assumption that voting is perfectly polarized such that members of a party, race, or ethnic group support only nominees of their group or party and that each group's voters are perfectly mobilized. We also assume that a group's votes are distributed evenly across their candidates when multiple candidates represent the optimal level of nomination. Values in parentheses represent surplus (or "wasted") votes—votes cast that do not contribute to the election of the group/party candidate(s). In practical terms, once a candidate receives votes beyond the minimum needed to elect an optimal number of the group's candidates, these "wasted" votes represent the votes that could be shared among additional candidates without diminishing the chances of electing the group's first candidate.

TABLE 3.2. Seats Won with Optimal Nominations under CV

Vote Share	Seats 2	3	4	5	6	7
10%	0 (10)	0 (10)	0 (10)	0 (10)	0 (10)	0 (10)
15%	0 (15)	0 (15)	0 (15)	0 (15)	1 (0.7)	1 (2.5)
20%	0 (20)	0 (20)	1 (0)	1 (3.4)	1 (5.7)	1 (7.5)
25%	0 (25)	1 (0)	1 (5)	1 (8.4)	1 (10.7)	2 (0)
30%	0 (30)	1 (5)	1 (10)	1 (13.4)	2 (1.4)	2 (5)
35%	1 (1.7)	1 (10)	1 (15)	2 (1.8)	2 (6.4)	2 (10)
40%	1 (6.7)	1 (15)	2 (0)	2 (6.8)	2 (11.4)	3 (2.5)
Threshold	33.3	25	20	16.6	14.3	12.5

Note: Nominations limited to *Vs/T*, rounded to lowest near integer. Cell entries represent the number of candidates that will be elected if the voting is perfectly polarized, voters are perfectly mobilized, there are no nomination errors, and the group's votes are divided evenly across nominated candidates. Values in parentheses are percentages of surplus votes.

For the purpose of illustration, the darker shaded area in the table represents those situations where under *optimal* nomination strategies, the slightest relaxation of discipline in bloc voting and voter mobilization would cause the group's candidate to lose if the candidate received no votes from other (nongroup) voters. The lightly shaded regions represent those situations where, under optimal nomination strategies, the slightest relaxation of discipline *and/or* slight relaxation of the additional assumption about perfect vote dispersion across the group's candidates could cause a candidate to lose. As the shaded areas in table 3.2 illustrate, there are numerous combinations of electoral schema and vote share that leave little margin for relaxation of these assumptions if the optimal number of candidates are to be elected. If, for example, the assumptions hold, with a group's vote share at 35 percent and five seats up, a shift of 1.8 percent of votes away from the group's candidates (or an equivalent loss via low mobilization) would, other things being equal, result in one less candidate being elected for the group.

· 4 ·

Elite Response to Cumulative Voting Election Rules

Ordinal electoral systems such as single transferable vote (STV), cumulative voting (CV), and limited voting (LV) demand substantial coordination of campaign activity on the part of candidates seeking office. Whether candidates, and especially minority candidates, can and do respond to the incentives created by these new electoral systems is a matter of some interest, since this has consequences both for minority representation and, more broadly still, for assessing the impact of institutions.

In changing electoral systems we should see changes in the incentive structures facing elites, which should, in turn, change their electioneering behavior. Some changes could lead to greater communication between candidates and voters, but others might not. Some changes could even affect a candidate's decision to enter the race in the first place. Electoral systems vary to the extent they encourage candidates for office to enter the contest, make themselves available, and make themselves known to citizens. Through the campaign process voters are not only made aware (or not) of the strengths and weaknesses of those candidates but also presented with an initial set of choices. Electoral systems thus give meaning to voters' choices by providing voters with a choice to begin with and also influencing how they see those alternatives.

Changes in the candidate pool brought about by changes in the electoral system can have subtle yet important effects on how—or even *if*—campaigns are contested. More candidates can mean more campaign activity on the part of parties, groups, or candidates, particularly if they are attempting to deal with the coordination problems outlined in the previous chapter. We assume that democratic processes are better served when elections are contested, when parties are organized to contest elections, and when candidates have incentives to campaign vigorously. If new election rules encourage previously disenfranchised (or politically discouraged) groups to contest elections, we should see that moves from single-member simple-plurality (SMSP) to more proportionate systems should precede increases in the number and variety of parties (candidates) either competing for office or winning seats in the legislature. In the next sections, we provide an overview of changes in candidate and party activities in jurisdictions that have switched from SMSP to proportional representation (PR) and CV/LV elections. We then move on to assess how these actors have responded to strategic coordination problems outlined in previous chapters.

As the examples in the previous chapters suggest, political parties are usually the actors who resolve coordination problems created by CV and LV systems. The nonpartisan nature of most local elections in the U.S. towns and cities where these systems have been employed makes the coordination process that much harder. These elections thus present an especially tough test case of the ability of electoral systems that demand serious organization of votes by candidates and of candidates themselves to improve minority representation.

Party and Candidate Mobilization in Response to New Election Rules

A change in election rules that lowers the threshold of exclusion should increase the pool of candidates who perceive that they have a chance of winning a seat. If the threshold is thought of as the minimum price of a seat, a lower threshold re-

FIGURE 4.1. Electoral System Change and Mobilization of Candidates: Morton Independent School District, Texas

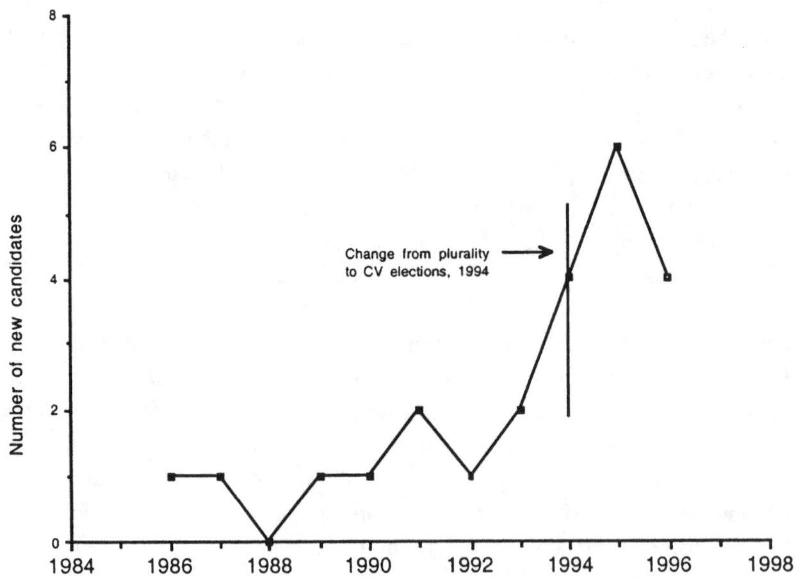

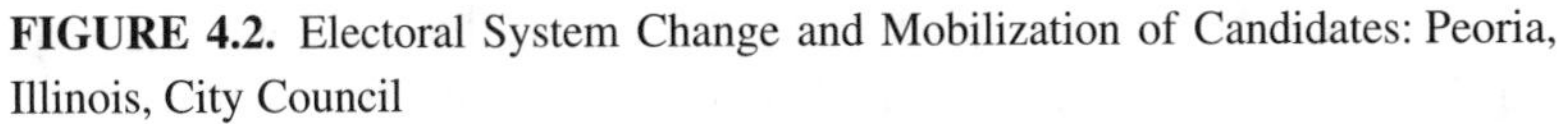
FIGURE 4.2. Electoral System Change and Mobilization of Candidates: Peoria, Illinois, City Council

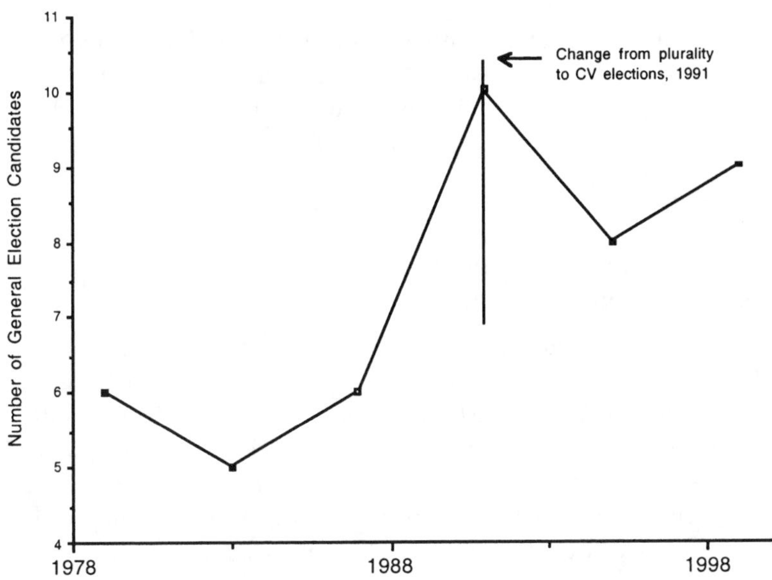

duces the potential cost of access to representation. This should mean that previously disenfranchised groups will recognize the new opportunities associated with the electoral process. For this reason, we expect that more parties and candidates will seek office after election rules are changed to lower the threshold of exclusion. CV and LV plans in the United States have all replaced plurality systems, and as such, establish a lower threshold that should lead to the mobilization of more candidates.

To illustrate this, we here examine how mobilization of parties and candidates is affected by election rules change in a number of contexts. Since CV is used in the United States in conjunction with nonpartisan elections, or partisan elections in a two-party system, we cannot, by definition, find evidence of new *parties* forming in response to CV or LV in such a setting. We can see similar effects for CV systems. Although parties may be absent in most CV elections, by lowering the threshold for seats, these rules have a similar effect on the mobilization of new candidates. Figure 4.1 shows the number of new candidates seeking office in one of the U.S. jurisdictions—the Morton, Texas, school district—switching from plurality at large to CV. Three or four seats from the seven-member board are elected each year in Morton. Across a series of elections prior to the switch to CV, no more than one or two new candidates challenged for a seat. In elections after CV was implemented, far more *new* candidates have sought office. A similar pattern can be seen in elections for the Peoria City Council (figure 4.2).[1] Wiggins and Petty (1979, 361) also found that

CV elections had a mobilizing effect on candidates in Illinois, largely because they caused more minority (party) candidates to enter contests, particularly in primaries.

In terms of raw numbers, these increases in candidate mobilization under CV may seem slight. But in low-salience local elections the mobilization of a few more candidates can make the difference between having a minority candidate on the ballot or not. In fact it can also make the difference between holding and canceling an election.

Party and Candidate Response to Vote Coordination Problems

The fact that candidates are mobilized does not, however, imply that they or their affiliated organizations are able to manage the coordination problems discussed in chapter 3. As we saw, voters can distribute their votes in many different ways in a multimember CV election. There are, in consequence, several different ways in which a candidate may stack up a winning vote total. Organization, nominating groups, and slating organizations are thus of key importance.

Is there systematic evidence to show this kind of organization taking place in U.S. local elections in the current period? After all, most U.S. jurisdictions adopting CV are nonpartisan, with the exception of some places in Alabama that use partisan ballots. Consequently, in most places there are no formal, enduring party organizations nominating candidates and campaigning on their behalf. This means not only that elections themselves do not take place in such a highly charged and partisan atmosphere but also that it is harder to form expectations over vote share so as to determine optimal nomination and vote dispersion strategies. But this does not imply that these communities lack enduring sources of cleavage. In every community included in our sample, CV was adopted to address issues of racial underrepresentation. These communities meet the U.S. Supreme Court's criteria for minority vote dilution: the minority groups are politically cohesive, and the majority group votes as a block to defeat minority candidates. Parties may be absent, but these communities nevertheless have sources of enduring cleavage (race) that may readily translate into expected vote shares for each group. Ethnic and racial divisions thus provide the basis for organizational capacity (nomination, slating, registration, campaigning) for some candidates.

Majority political organizations are often altogether absent in U.S. local elections (Adrian 1952; Williams and Adrian 1963). Prewitt (1970) noted that "nonpolitical" civic associations and probusiness groups—established and supported by upper-middle-class whites—assume a large role in local races in lieu of parties (see also Logan and Molotch 1987). These groups can virtually assume the role of a party when they control and publicize candidate slates, recruit candidates, and mobilize voters. Davidson and Fraga (1988) demonstrated that slating groups have exercised great influence in nonpartisan elections in midsized Texas cities. In mature form, they are essentially parties of the white business class (387).

Of course, the central question is whether poorer and minority voters and candidates have access to organizational vehicles that can be used at election time. In principle, minority and nonbusiness populations do have access to organizations that may supply a substitute for parties (Voting Rights Act suit plaintiffs groups, Parent-Teacher Association groups, "good government" civic associations or grassroots ethnic associations such as the National Association for the Advancement of Colored People for African Americans or, for Latinos, the League of United Latin American Citizens [LULAC]). All these kinds of groups could in principle provide the means of organizing and coordinating voters. Whether groups, and especially groups supporting minority candidates, can actually organize voters in practice is thus an empirical question. It is also an important one given that CV is supposed to be a remedy for minority underrepresentation and that it is plausible to suppose that minority groups are organizationally disadvantaged and hence likely to be especially disadvantaged by a system such as CV.

Research Design

As we noted above, claiming that specific effects are due to electoral system changes is one thing, but being able to demonstrate that such effects exist and are due to electoral institutions and not, say, to distinct cultural patterns can be quite another. To get at some of these questions of organization and coordination in contemporary CV elections, we surveyed candidates seeking local offices under CV in 1996 and 1997 to measure how candidates, their affiliated groups, and political parties behaved when contesting elections. We also surveyed candidates seeking offices in at-large plurality and SMSP districts in a similar set of communities from within the same region; this allowed us to compare candidate attitudes and behaviors across two different institutional settings but within very similar racial and cultural contexts (see Appendix B). The survey included questions about the candidates' campaign activities, their electoral histories, and campaigning, slating, and voter registration activities that organizations might have engaged in on their behalf. In addition to standard demographic questions, we asked candidates about attempts at communicating voter dispersion/plumping strategies.

The survey results give us some reason for thinking that candidates, even minority candidates in nonpartisan elections, were able to meet the organizational

TABLE 4.1. Candidate Vote Apportionment Strategies in U.S. Local CV Elections

Asked of candidates running under CV: Did you ask voters to:

	White	Minority	Total	N
Plump	27.0	61.5	31.0	35
Give you some votes	15.0	23.1	15.9	18
Divide between you and other	5.0	0.0	4.4	5
No instructions	53.0	15.4	48.7	55
No. of respondents	100	13	100.0	113

demands of the CV system. At first glance, however, the patterns can seem hard to find. Our surveys of candidates contesting local CV elections in the United States found that 80 percent of respondents indicated that their own personal campaigns were not linked to other candidates' efforts. Few reported that their own campaigns included vote coordination strategies designed to elect multiple candidates. Nevertheless, a substantial proportion did reveal that affiliated groups worked to mobilize voters and communicate vote strategies. Most CV candidates also reported their own campaigns used ads, literature, or mailing to communicate with voters, and half of these said their materials included some information about how voters should distribute their votes.

Table 4.1 illustrates that over half of our respondents claimed to articulate some vote dispersion or plumping strategy in their conversations with voters. Minority candidates in particular told voters to plump, while white candidates were more likely to solicit some but not all votes. The same pattern holds when we look at how candidates communicated with their individual ads, mailings, and literature. Additional cross-tabulations (not reported) demonstrate that *groups* endorsing minority candidates were more likely to ask voters to plump than groups endorsing white candidates. This makes sense given the strategic incentives associated with CV systems (see chapter 3).

Table 4.2 shows that when CV candidates were asked if a group was working to communicate vote strategies on behalf of their *opponents* one-third said yes, with 20 percent indicating that the groups communicated vote dispersion (rather than plumping) strategies on behalf of their opponents. While few reported communicating that they themselves had coordinated vote dispersion with other can-

TABLE 4.2. Endorsing Group Vote Apportionment Strategies in U.S. Local CV Elections

Asked of candidates running under CV: If a group worked for your opponent, did the . . .

	Percent	Number
endorsing group tell voters to divide their votes	19.0	21
group endorse one candidate and told voters to plump	12.6	14
group endorse, but didn't say how to distribute votes	9.9	11
other	9.0	10
there was no group giving an endorsement	49.5	55
total		111

didates, one-fifth of our respondents indicated that a group had been organized to conduct such vote coordination for their opponents.[2]

Candidates appealing to a smaller group of voters (minorities) engaged in plumping, while those from larger groups (white) were more likely to be associated with vote dispersion strategies. This finding is also seen in case studies of CV elections in the United States. Bobby Agee, the first black candidate elected in Chilton County, Alabama, recognized the importance of plumping in his first election and actively advocated a plumping strategy in his 1988 campaign. Pildes and Donoghue (1995, 273) reported that his ads asked voters for all seven of their votes.[3] Yet in 1988 African American Democratic Party organizations (the Alabama Democratic Conference and the New South Coalition [NSC]) distributed sample ballots that advised voters to give only one vote each to the party's seven council candidates. It seems, however, that both of these party organizations soon "learned" the importance of coordinating the African American vote. The 1992 NSC sample ballot advised seven votes for Agee (who was reelected), and the 1994 NSC sample ballot advised voters to divide their votes between two black candidates. The strategy advised giving a black incumbent three votes while sending four to a black challenger, Edward Reed. Reed won a seat, and the incumbent was defeated (sample ballots reproduced in Pildes and Donoghue 1995, 312–13).

Our survey results also demonstrate that even where parties are absent, minority candidates and minority political organizations act to communicate plumping strategies. A single-sheet campaign ad for Inez Moncada, the first minority candidate elected by CV in the United States, demonstrates this vividly. One of Moncada's campaign ads from the 1987 Alamogordo City Council election included five distinct appeals for voters to plump all three of their votes on her ballot line, including this request:

> My promise to you is that I will not vote for any higher taxes. If you feel the same way, I would appreciate you pulling all three levers above my name. . . . DON'T DILUTE YOUR VOTE! CAST THREE VOTES FOR LOWER TAXES. (Engstrom, Taebel, and Cole 1989, 486. Emphasis in original)

Despite the relatively low salience of these U.S. local elections, and even in the absence of parties, experience demonstrates that parties and candidates are often quick to respond to the vote coordination problems associated with CV in these local elections. Below, we assess how this might make campaigning more vigorous under CV than other systems, and we examine how voters respond to these appeals.

Registration and Voter Mobilization

As in any election campaign, candidates increase their chances of election by mobilizing potential supporters. Campaign activity is particularly important in CV contests since it needs to be a vehicle for addressing vote coordination problems as well as a method for mobilizing voters to turnout. If no one coordinates the number of candidates that a group lists on the ballot, or coordinates vote dispersion or mobilizes voters, then CV elections are not necessarily going to produce electoral outcomes proportional to a given share of the population.

In CV elections, demands for candidate organizational capacity are furthered by the need to register and mobilize potential supporters. The strategic demands of CV discussed in chapter 3 demonstrate that turnout must be maximized for groups to win their optimal seat share. Moreover, empirical research demonstrates that minority groups having voting strength at or near the threshold of exclusion achieve representation under CV only if turnout equals or exceeds that of whites (Brischetto and Engstrom 1997). Under SMSP districted elections, minority-group and/or party supporters are often concentrated into a spatial area, ensuring that they will secure descriptive representation even if their turnout levels are relatively low. With a plurality at-large system, nonmajority groups have little incentive to contest elections since they stand little chance of winning

TABLE 4.3. Group Mobilization Activity in U.S. Local CV and Plurality Elections

Asked of candidates running under CV: Were groups in the community working actively to register and mobilize voters on your behalf?

	White CV Candidates	Minority CV Candidates	All CV Candidates
Yes	14.8%	33.3%	17.1%
No	85.2%	66.7%	82.0%
Total:	108%	15%	123%
		Chi-square = 3.19, $p < .07$	

Note: Cell entries are column percentages.

Asked of candidates running under CV: Were groups in the community working actively to register and mobilize voters on your opponent's behalf?

	White CV Candidates	Minority CV Candidates	All CV Candidates
Yes	35.9%	14.3%	33.3%
No	64.1%	85.7%	66.7%
Total:	103%	14%	117%
		Chi-square = 2.59, $p < .10$	

a seat. For these reasons, we expect that more groups will work to mobilize voters in places using CV than in places using plurality election rules.

Table 4.3 displays the results of candidate perceptions about group activity in these jurisdictions. It is not surprising that most respondents claim that no groups were working to register and mobilize on their behalf or that of their opponents (82 percent and 66 percent, respectively); these are, after all, low-salience elections in primarily small rural communities. Yet there is a surprising amount of mobilization efforts in these CV communities—particularly on behalf of minority candidates. One-third of minority candidates reported groups working actively to register voters on their behalf, and just over one-third of white candidates reported organizations working actively to register voters on behalf of their opponents. Nonpartisan groups mentioned by respondents included LULAC, labor unions, teachers, and chambers of commerce. Broadly similar patterns are found with respect to vote management activities. In addition to voter mobilization and registration (noted above), we asked specifically whether respondents were assisted by organizations that coordinated vote strategies, issued endorsements, or spent money on their behalf.

These results are consistent with Brischetto's description of the CV campaign environment in the sixteen Texas communities he studied in 1995. He noted the important role that minority groups played in organizing their communities and in emphasizing turnout. In Atlanta, Texas, blacks used door-to-door get-out-the-vote efforts in black neighborhoods during that city's school district election. In Morton, Roscoe, and Rotan, the Southwest Voter Registration Education Project "provided training in voter mobilization under cumulative voting" (Brischetto 1995, 351–52). In Yorktown, Concerned Citizens for Voting began mobilizing Latino voters in that city's first CV election in 1991 (Brischetto 1995, 352).

Organization and Group Campaign Activity on Behalf of Candidates

Despite some mobilization activity in CV places, the visible role of political organizations appears to be somewhat limited in these local contests. Forty-one percent of CV candidates said their opponents were endorsed by "some group," but only 8.5 percent indicated that they themselves ran either as a part of "a group of candidates sharing similar views" or as part of an endorsing group's slate.

Beyond the mobilization efforts and extension of endorsements, it is difficult to identify extensive extracandidate organizational activity. Few candidates reported that the endorsing group also campaigned on their behalf. Minority candidates were in fact far more likely to report having received an endorsement from a political organization. Sixty-one percent of minority CV candidates ran with endorsements, while only 13 percent of Anglos candidates did (chi-square 15.6, $p < .001$). As both Bridges (1997) and Davidson and Fraga (1988) demonstrated, for low-information nonpartisan settings, the power of such endorsements can nevertheless transcend any amount of actual campaigning.

Overall, minority candidates were more dependent upon endorsements for victory. Fifty-seven percent of the endorsed minorities won elections, but not a single minority candidate was elected without a group's endorsement. Conversely, Anglo candidates were elected at high rates regardless of having received endorsements (70 percent of those endorsed were elected vs. 81 percent of those not endorsed who were elected). Although nonpartisan political organizations might have a somewhat limited overall role in assisting CV campaigns, these data suggest that minority candidates require endorsing organizations to win.

All of this suggests that candidates from majority and minority groups may benefit from organized campaign activities in different ways, but this would seem to be related not so much to ethnic status per se as to the number of candidates. Minorities, in particular, relied upon group endorsements and some campaigning on their behalf by organizations. Though relatively few are in our sample, none won and few sought office without a group's assistance. Consistent with the coordination problems minorities face under CV, groups backing minorities were more likely to ask voters to plump. On the other hand, the few candidates who participated in multicandidate slates were white, and these were the only respondents who claimed to use vote apportionment strategies.

Individual Candidate Campaign Activities under CV

Despite the small size of most of these communities, there is some evidence of active campaigning on the part of individual candidates. The average candidate spent only about $600, and this figure is highly skewed by a few relatively big spenders. Many spent less than $100. Candidates reported that most of their own campaign money was spent on newspaper ads, signs, mailings, and radio ads. The most common campaign activities included paying for advertisements in local newspapers (50 percent of CV respondents), telephoning (36 percent), meeting with newspaper editors and reporters (32 percent), and speaking at public forums (36 percent).

Some of the candidates' individual campaign activity is not necessarily associated with success, in part because challengers seem to campaign harder in attempting to overcome incumbents. Winning CV candidates—a large proportion who were incumbents—spent less ($\bar{X}$ = $528) on average than CV losers ($\bar{X}$ = $735). We also examined two other measures of campaign activities that showed no significant differences between winners and losers. On a five-point subjective measure of overall activity relative to opponents, losing candidates thought their campaigns were slightly more active ($t = 1.18$, $p < .22$). An objective index we constructed that summarizes responses to questions about 10 separate campaign activities[4] found losers reporting slightly more activities (2.6) than winners (2.2, $t = 0.92$, $p < .36$).

These differences are associated both with incumbency and with race. Incumbents reported that their campaigns were less active than other candidates. Nonincumbents mentioned an average of 2.7 activities, compared to 1.6 for incumbents ($t = 2.52$, $p < .01$). Nonincumbents were also more likely to spend money on ads. Yet nearly all incumbents responding to our survey were elected regardless of their level of campaign activity. Among white challengers, 70 percent of active candidates (those above the mean in campaign activities) won their election, compared to 59 percent of less active white candidates. In contrast, nearly all minority candidates (90 percent) were nonincumbents, and minorities reported more campaign activities ($\bar{X} = 3.0$) than whites ($\bar{X} = 2.2$, $t = 1.15$, $p < .26$). Among minority challengers, 50 percent of active candidates won, compared to 20 percent of less active candidates. Individual campaign activity under CV thus appears particularly important to nonincumbents, and also for minority candidates.

Discussion

To date, there have been few empirical studies of how candidates contest CV elections. Examples of CV electoral practice and results from our surveys illustrate that even in local elections held in small communities where elections are largely nonpartisan, candidates and affiliated organizations respond to the demands of CV election systems. Their response to these demands, in the form of voter mobilization and attempts to solve vote coordination problems, shed some light on how CV systems might potentially produce proportional descriptive representation along the lines of dominant community cleavages—in this case, race. Without some sort of effective mediation by political organizations, and without active campaigns by candidates, proportionate group representation under plans such as CV and LV can be spoiled by over- or undernomination, problems of vote dispersion, and low turnout. The findings here suggest that even in the near-total absence of political parties, CV elections appear to beget candidate activities and organizations that structure campaigns—if only loosely.

These findings also provide an empirical illustration of the critical role played by campaign activities in CV elections. Although districting plans that use homogeneous minority districts may facilitate descriptive minority representation regardless of registration and turnout differentials, and with less concern for strategic campaign activity, CV systems may not mitigate such majority-group advantages automatically. While CV presents a challenge to minority groups, it also presents an opportunity. While CV does provide organizational barriers to candidates and groups, they are clearly not insuperable ones. Indeed, one interpretation is that since CV creates incentives for organization to occur it encourages greater involvement and participation in politics more generally. Guinier (1991; 1993) and others have popularized the idea that CV improves upon race-based districting by facilitating greater minority influence over all representatives rather than only those elected by majority-minority districts.

We suggest that by making demands for vote coordination, candidate recruitment, and vote mobilization, CV plans might also invigorate local politics as political organizations and candidates resolve to meet these demands. In the following chapter we look more closely at two key issues of process. We assess how the competitiveness of elections and the conduct of campaigns differ between CV and plurality communities. We then look at how voters respond to the vote coordination strategies communicated by CV campaigns. After establishing that these micro-level mechanisms are present in CV elections, we turn our attention to how these factors might cause differences in turnout and representation between CV/LV and plurality places.

· 5 ·

Election Rules and Political Campaigns

So far we have established that it is reasonable to expect that candidates under CV will need to organize more than candidates under rival systems such as the single-member districted (SMD) systems. Other things being equal, then, we expect that this level of organization and contest will translate into candidates' campaigning more vigorously under CV than under plurality elections. That is, there should be behavioral consequences of changing electoral rules that should result in more, and quite possibly different, electioneering by candidates under CV than other systems.

In all arguments of this kind, the difficulty lies in being able to demonstrate a link between changes in behavior—here campaigning—and institutional factors. Here, we took fuller advantage of our comparative case selection (see chapter 1 above and Appendix C for a fuller discussion). By administering a survey of campaign activity to candidates seeking offices in both CV and non-CV communities, we could begin to compare campaign activity with respect to institutional structures. It allowed us to use candidate perceptions to see, for example, if there were indeed more groups working to mobilize voters under CV rules than under non-CV rules. It is important to underscore that by matching the selection of CV and non-CV cases we could be more confident that any differences in campaign activity would be attributable to electoral rules rather than contextual or political differences between jurisdictions.

One complicating measurement issue that we address below lies in finding an appropriate measure of campaign activity and vigor. Unfortunately, we lack clear theoretical priors that would help us to identify campaign acts that are more important than others. Candidates can do many kinds of things during an election: Which ones should we pick out or otherwise emphasize? On the face of it, we would expect attending campaign meetings and attending public events to be better indicators of campaign effort than simply handing out some buttons or bumper stickers. On the other hand, both handing out bumper stickers and holding town hall meetings are indicators of *some* effort being made by a candidate and so cannot be ignored. Clearly, some kind of summary measure would help us here in tapping into the activities and expenditures that more directly disseminate information to voters about the candidate.

The Electoral System and Competition for Office

Since we assumed that vote coordination and mobilization demands would require that CV candidates or associated organizations might need to work "harder," we asked all candidates about their campaign activities. As noted in the previous chapter, we created an index, summarizing the number of activities they claimed to be doing, that we intended to represent a "first cut" at measuring campaign activity. We also asked if groups worked in their community to register voters, if organizations endorsed them, and if organizations worked to assist their own campaign. As an additional measure of political activity by organizations, we asked candidates if they perceived that groups or organizations endorsed or worked for their opponents. We also asked candidates about their campaign spending and had them answer a subjective question comparing their level of campaign activity to their opponent's activity.

We found only mixed evidence that CV elections were associated with distinctively vigorous campaigns. After dividing respondents into three categories—those seeking office under CV, under SMSP districts, and under standard-plurality at-large elections—and using the additive index as a measure of campaign activity, we found no difference between candidates seeking office under CV and those seeking office under other election systems. As illustrated in table 5.1, an ANOVA test comparing candidates running in CV places to those running in other places showed no difference in the mean levels of activities reported under each election system.[1] The table also shows that there were no significant differences in campaign spending or subjective impressions of personal campaign activity across systems.

There are, however, some things to suggest that local CV elections might be more likely to trigger the involvement of political organizations that work to increase voter participation. As table 5.1 illustrates, candidates seeking office under CV were significantly more likely to report that political organizations worked actively to register voters. Thus, responses to this question indicate that campaigning under CV is different—political organizations may be more involved in mobilizing and registering voters in CV campaigns. This finding makes sense given the assumptions about coordination problems discussed in chapter 3.

At first glance, some of these results seem more than a little underwhelming. It seems that we have to look quite hard to find serious evidence of effects of the

TABLE 5.1. CV Candidate and Plurality Candidate Campaign Activity Compared

Indicator of Campaign Activity	Value for CV Place	Value for SMD Place	Value for At-Large Place	Test Statistic	Prob.
Mean number of campaign activities	2.4 (115)	2.6 (50)	2.5 (89)	ANOVA	n.s.
Average candidate spending	$600 (112)	$784 (42)	$867 (71)	ANOVA	n.s.
Subjective ranking of activity (mean)[a]	3.3 (122)	3.3 (44)	3.3 (93)	ANOVA	n.s.
Candidate ran as part of a slate (%)	7.9 (122)	8.5 (47)	6.5 (93)	Chi-square	n.s.
Groups working to register voters (%)	33.3 (117)	22.2 (44)	20.6 (86)	Chi-square	$p < .08$
Total in group:	126	51	103		

Note: Number of respondents in parentheses, n.s. = not significant difference.

[a]Self-reported ranking of campaign activity ranging from 1 (far more active than others) to 5 (far less active than others).

electoral system upon campaign activities. But there is one fundamental way in which we can see how the electoral system shapes elections, and does so in a manner that helps to account for the underwhelming results of table 5.1. A closer examination of the information about campaign activities indicates that a substantial proportion of candidates who reported campaign activities in plurality jurisdictions "campaigned" without opposition. This is particularly evident in candidate responses from communities using SMD elections.

Districted elections can often produce safe seats that no challenger can reasonably hope to successfully contest, leaving incumbents to campaign unopposed. On the other hand, CV offers incentives for more candidates to mobilize and seek office because challengers are likely to perceive that they have a higher chance of winning. Everything else being equal, then, we should see more contested elections under CV than in districted systems. As we can see from table 5.2, this is indeed the case, and quite dramatically so.

As table 5.2 illustrates, none of the candidates responding to our survey from CV jurisdictions were unopposed when they sought office, while thirty-one candidates in non-CV places (15 percent of the total) reported that they faced no opposition. Forty-three percent of candidates seeking districted seats were unopposed, as were 14.7 percent in standard at-large places.[2]

TABLE 5.2. Percent of Candidates without Challengers, by Election System

Candidate status	Cumulative voting	Single-member district	At-large plurality	Total % (N)
unopposed (%)	00.0	43.1	16.2	15.6 (33)
opposed (%)	100.0	56.9	83.8	84.4 (178)
Total	92	51	68	211

Note: chi-square = 46.2; significant at $p < .0001$

The results in table 5.2 probably overstate the effect that electoral system has on competition for local office. After all, not all CV elections during the period of our study were contested. In interviews with local officials, we identified a small number of CV elections where candidates were unopposed in 1996. Nevertheless, our interviews with local officials and these survey data indicate that SMD elections are much more likely to lack opposing candidates than CV elections.

It is, of course, possible that this effect is a function of the newness or novelty of CV elections. CV could have a short-term effect on mobilization of new candidates, who, having tried once under the new CV rules, potentially withdraw from politics later or become safe incumbents who subsequently deter challengers. But the boost from novelty should also apply to those communities that have adopted districting in place of at-large elections. Yet it is not seen in these communities.

Even with these caveats in mind, we suggest that the relationship between electoral system and electoral competition demonstrated in table 5.2 is too substantial to dismiss and that any overstatement of effect is quite small. Thus, on one fundamental criterion used to define a well-functioning democracy, contested elections, we see what may be a crucial effect of election rules.

The figures of table 5.2 also help us to understand some of the null findings of table 5.1. The set of elections we are comparing will be quite different from each other along a notional dimension of competitiveness. Districted elections are either not contested at all or potentially extremely competitive, with, at a minimum, two candidates (c_{min}) jockeying for one seat (m). Along some notional dimension of competitiveness, then, districted elections are distributed bimodally, being either very competitive or very uncompetitive. By contrast, far fewer CV elections are uncontested, since having one candidate more than seats at stake causes all CV candidates to be "opposed." But to arrive at the same level of competitiveness as districted elections, $2m$ candidates would have to run (e.g., six candidates in a three-seat contest). To match the "two candidates for every seat" level of competitiveness that might occur if a SMD race was actually contested, a three-seat CV election would have to attract six candidates. However, a CV election is contested at $c_{min} = m + 1$, not $2m$. In attracting "only" four or five candidates, the three-seat CV election may not be as competitive as a *contested* SMD race and may not generate as much campaign activity.

The two different electoral settings thus produce two very different distributions of campaign activity: CV elections that show a moderate degree of competitiveness across all cases and districted cases that either hold no election or host a very competitive one. Since, by definition, we are comparing campaign activity in some districts where $c_{min} = 2m$ elections took place, we are comparing active candidates from the most competitive districted elections ($c_{min} = 2m$) to all of the candidates from CV elections ($c_{min} = m + 1$). If anything, this selection bias should work against the hypothesis of more competitive CV elections and, in fact, should produce patterns that show significantly higher levels of campaign activity for districted elections.

The Electoral System and Campaign Expenditure

As electoral systems might affect the scope of campaigning, they might also affect the cost of campaigns. Campaign costs and expenditures can be seen as one measure of how much effort candidates are making to reach voters (Palda 1994; Lupia and Gerber 1995). Campaign expenditures can also be seen as the size of the bet candidates need to place in order to play and so can be seen not just as a measure of effort but also as a measure of entry barriers—barriers that may be especially hard for challengers (and minorities) to overcome. Both interpretations of campaign expenditures—as the size of the hurdle candidates face and as the measure of information transmitted—can be found in the literature. Standard at-large plans and CV require that candidates target voters over an entire jurisdiction, while SMD allows candidates to concentrate their resources within a smaller, less populated area and hence demands fewer resources to begin with. Indeed, Pildes and Donoughue (1995) reported that minority plaintiffs in Alabama feared that CV elections, being contested countywide, would cost more than district races and thus disadvantage minority candidates.[3] It was important, then, for us to know whether an electoral system change was "expenditure neutral," since any system that leads to higher costs for seeking office can affect the pool of candidates who can mount credible campaigns.

We tested for the effect of election rules on campaign spending by estimating candidate expenditure as a function of electoral system, controlling for the size of the jurisdiction,[4] the candidate's race/ethnicity, and various indicators of candidate advantages that might reduce or affect the need to spend money to win (incumbency, and running opposed vs. unopposed). We also included a variable indicating that a candidate won his or her race as a post hoc surrogate for candidate quality. Two dummy variables, one that contrasted candidates from SMD

TABLE 5.3. Estimations of Campaign Spending, by Election System. Dependent variable equals dollars of expenditure.

Variables	Model 1	Model 2	Model 3	Model 4	Model 5
CV place	–23.2	–183.2	–136.5	–192.5	–238.9
	(277)	(307.3)	(318.5)	(310.8)	(321.1)
SMD place	—	–491.7[a]	–472.4	–488.4[a]	–455.7+
		(361.3)	(366.3)	(363.2)	(358.6)
Minority candidate	–648.0+	–605.4	–610.4+	–608.1[a]	–589.4
	(383.4)	(383.1)	(393.5)	(384.9)	(385.7)
Small place	–3059.9**	–3165.1**	–3066.0**	–3142.5**	–3083.5**
	(404.9)	(411.2)	(427.9)	(418.1)	(432.5)
Winner	—	—	–60.7	—	—
			(65.1)		
Incumbent	—	—	—	–84.5	—
				(275.5)	
Opposed	—	—	—	—	255.5
					(410.5)
Constant	7157.2**	7512.8**	7357.6**	7517.8**	6878.1**
	(871.3)	(904.1)	(933.9)`	(906.2)	(1363.8)
Adj. R^2	.23	.24	.24	.25	.23
Number of cases	194	194	191	194	194

Note: Unstandardized OLS coefficients. Standard errors in parentheses.

** = $p < .01$, two-tailed.
* = $p < .05$, two-tailed.
+ = $p < .05$, one-tailed.
[a] = $p < .10$, one-tailed.

places with standard at-large plurality places and one that contrasted CV and at-large plurality candidates, represented measures of the electoral system. Since a standard at-large system requires a candidate to win a plurality jurisdiction-wide, we expected SMD and CV candidates to spend less.

Campaign expenditure was determined in our survey. Results of our estimations of campaign spending (for candidates reporting spending more than $10) are displayed in table 5.3. These estimations explain roughly one-quarter of the variance in the candidates' reported expenditure and suggest that CV campaigns are not more expensive than plurality at-large campaigns.[5] Compared to all other systems, an at-large system modified with CV is not associated with greater campaign spending. The dummy variable representing SMD systems, however, does produce significant effects in some models. When we control for incumbency and for candidates claiming to be unopposed, we find that candidates in SMD races do spend less than candidates who seek office under at-large systems. This is consistent with the argument that at-large elections imply a bigger area and a larger number of voters to cover. The most consistent expenditure effect is not surprising: candidates in smaller communities spend substantially less than other candidates. Minority candidates also appear to spend less when community size, electoral system, and electoral success are held constant.

In terms of the conduct of political campaigns, our results suggest that CV elections are in many ways quite promising from a participatory perspective. Under CV rules, elections are more likely to be contested and are more likely to involve organizations that try to mobilize voters; further, while campaign costs are probably higher under CV than under SMD, CV campaigns are not more expensive when compared to other at-large plans. Since nearly all places adopting CV are switching from at-large elections, they will probably find no increase in the costs of campaigning brought about by new election rules. Finding some evidence of increased competitiveness under CV (as in tables 5.1 and 5.2) without increased cost is quite plausible, since these are relatively small communities where high-cost election technology is rarely used to begin with. Still, these data also suggest that a standard at-large jurisdiction facing a choice between CV and SMD might find SMD attractive, since it could possibly produce lower campaign costs than exist under a standard at-large system.

The pattern of results in tables 5.1 through 5.3 suggests that we have to look for more subtle distinctions of campaign activity between these election systems. In the next section, we examine how other factors associated with campaign style might make CV a more attractive alternative than SMD. Apart from finding certain elements of competitive campaigning under CV (contested elections, involvement of organizations, no decrease in spending as seen in SMD), we have not really identified whether there is a distinct "style" of campaigning under CV. Using factor analysis, we can begin to identify unique dimensions of campaign style that might be associated with different electoral systems.

Campaign Activity in Local Elections

While campaign expenditures may represent a good proxy measure for overall effort, dollar totals do not always reflect what candidates actually *do* during the course of an election. It would be good, especially given our emphasis on process, to try to establish what kinds of electioneering candidates engage in. Here the candidate surveys can provide some supporting detail. Among the questions we asked candidates were one set of 10 questions measuring general activities and another set of sixteen questions measuring how candidates spent their money (on signs or mailings or newspaper ads, radio ads and so on).

As we noted above, there seems to be little prior theory to lead us to expect that candidates should focus on posting yard signs to the exclusion of other activities or attend meetings rather than giving out bumper stickers. A factor analysis of responses to this battery of questions would allow us to identify any overarching structure to the array of activities that candidates pursue (if any). For our purpose, factor analysis operates on the assumption that these individual activities are representative of some larger, unobserved dimensions of campaign activity (Kim and Muller 1978, 25). If there is a smaller set of dimensions, or campaign styles, that candidates might employ in local races, factor analysis will reveal the activities that have the most in common with each dimension. It also allows us to give each individual candidate a score on the dimension—or factor—representing particular styles of campaigning as a means of assessing certain kinds of activities.

We included all twenty-six candidate activity items from our survey in this factor analysis and report the results in table 5.4. The analysis produced eight distinct factors with eigenvalues over 1.0 and explained 67 percent of the total variance in the items. The fifth and subsequent factors were largely represented by single items (i.e., only one item loaded at over .40), so we list only the first four in the table. Table 5.4 lists scores that are analogous to each activity's correlation with a particular dimension of campaigning. Those that load most significantly on a factor are expressed in bold. The first four factors explain over 48 percent of the variance and have multiple items loading on each factor.

The factors are clearly distinct in terms of the items that they encompass. Compared to the other major factors here, the first and largest factor (factor 1) appears to be a dimension of campaign activities that requires a fair amount of personal activity on the part of the candidate (meetings, interviews, speaking). With this style of campaigning, candidates also spend their (limited) funds exclusively on advertising in the form of signs, mailings, radio and print ads, and brochures. In contrast, the second and third factors appear to represent styles of campaigning that rely less on personal activity on the part of the candidate and more on paid office staff (factor 2) or paid consultants and social events (factor 3). The style of campaigning identified by factor 4 is reflected in walking precincts and spending on signs, brochures, and paid staff.

None of this, as we noted at the outset, is terribly theoretical. It also suffers from all the usual caveats attendant on using factor analysis. Nevertheless, it does help us to identify some clusters of electioneering activity actually engaged in by candidates, and we can use this measure of activity, rather than some summary dollar total, to examine candidate activity under different electoral regimes. How candidates spend can vary quite markedly. Take, for example, fac-

TABLE 5.4. Factor Analysis of Candidate Campaign Activity

Activities/Expenses	Factor 1	Factor 2	Factor 3	Factor 4
Knock on doors	0.262	0.128	–0.067	0.295
Walk precincts	0.085	0.133	0.019	**0.460**
Speak publicly	**0.669**	0.129	0.121	0.173
Letters to editors	**0.402**	–0.103	0.057	–0.058
Meet editors/reporters	**0.746**	0.130	0.150	0.210
Meetings w/ supporters	**0.639**	0.134	0.266	–0.055
Telephone supporters	0.154	0.081	0.154	–0.073
Organize social events	0.233	0.023	**0.629**	–0.013
Paid for advertising	**0.563**	0.098	0.020	0.009
Paid for campaign staff	–0.016	**0.820**	0.356	0.115
Spent on signs	**0.605**	0.133	0.036	**0.438**
Spent on mail	**0.636**	–0.063	0.226	0.150
Spent on radio	**0.777**	–0.084	0.059	–0.005
Spent on newspaper	**0.503**	–0.042	0.096	0.068
Spent on TV	0.321	–0.021	–0.064	–0.130
Spent on brochures	**0.508**	–0.010	0.068	**0.461**
Spent on bumper stickers	0.160	0.034	–0.019	–0.006
Spent on food for volunteers	0.286	0.071	**0.434**	0.358
Spent on phone	0.188	0.076	**0.727**	–0.084
Spent on misc items w/ name	0.049	0.052	0.240	0.090
Spent on precinct data	0.093	–0.026	0.027	0.112
Spent on staff/personnel	0.182	0.000	0.164	**0.823**
Spent on office space	0.071	**0.748**	**0.402**	0.058
Spent on legal services	0.079	0.357	**0.689**	0.121
Spent on political consultant	–0.120	0.303	**0.750**	0.207
Spent on buttons	0.106	**0.897**	–0.173	0.071
Percent of total variance explained:	27.4	10.1	6.3	5.4

Note: Rotated factor loadings. Items loading at .40 or greater are in **boldface**.

tor 1, which identifies clusters of campaign activity that involve labor-intensive, direct, and active contact with voters. Efforts of this kind may be poorly reflected by campaign spending measures, yet it would be hard to argue that they do not count as campaigning. Moreover, it is plausible that labor-intensive campaigns are exactly the kind of campaigns that poor and/or minority challengers are more likely to use. Differences in campaign activity across the range of actions identified by the first factor in table 5.4 are therefore of particular interest. Thus, while we have no wish to make too many claims on behalf of the factor-analytic approach, it does help to provide a somewhat more rounded picture of electioneering under different electoral systems than one provided by simply looking at expenditures.

TABLE 5.5. Estimations of Campaign "Style" (Dependent Variable = Factor Scores from Factor 1, Table 4)

Variables	Model 1	Model 2	Model 3	Model 4	Model 5
CV place	.308[**]	.219[*]	.225[+]	.210[+]	.201[+]
	(.115)	(.127)	(.130)	(.125)	(.121)
SMD place	—	–.247[+]	–.242[+]	–.223[a]	–.185
		(.148)	(.150)	(.148)	(.157)
Minority candidate	–.212[a]	–.197	–.223[a]	–.198	–.185
	(.157)	(.157)	(.161)	(.156)	(.157)
Small place	–1.70[**]	–1.75[**]	–1.72[**]	–1.69[**]	–1.69[**]
	(.171)	(1.73)	(.179)	(.175)	(.181)
Winner	—	—	–.016	—	—
			(.028)		
Incumbent	—	—	—	–.193[+]	—
				(.113)	
Opposed	—	—	—	—	.202
					(.171)
Constant	3.29[**]	3.45[**]	3.45[**]	3.45[**]	2.95[**]
	(.36)	(.39)	(.38)	(.37)	(.56)
Adj. R2	.32	.33	.33	.34	.33
Number of cases	211	211	208	211	211

Note: Unstandardized OLS coefficients. Standard errors in parentheses.

** = $p < .01$, two-tailed.
* = $p < .05$, two-tailed.
+ = $p < .05$, one-tailed.
a = $p < .10$, one-tailed.

One straightforward approach is to generate factor scores for each candidate based on the dimensions of campaign style displayed in table 5.4. We can then use this factor score as a dependent variable in models identical to those employed in our estimations of expenditure (table 5.3). In doing this, we found that the type of electoral system does have an impact, at least so far as activity along the first dimension of campaign activity is concerned. The estimations of candidate scores on factor 1, displayed in table 5.5, illustrate that our models explain about one-third of the variation in candidate scores on this style of campaigning.

Table 5.5 illustrates that even when we control for the size of jurisdictions, incumbency status, minority status, the presence of opposition, and whether the candidate won, we find that candidates seeking office in CV places are significantly more likely to score high on the direct, active style of campaigning represented by factor 1. As is consistent with the argument that bigger districts require more effort, this style of campaigning is also most pronounced in large places. We also see that challengers are, on the whole, more active than are incumbents.

These results are consistent with expectations that CV campaigns may stimulate (or require) a certain increase in the level of activity on the part of candidates facing the need to communicate vote strategies to supporters who are dispersed across an entire jurisdiction. The results in table 5.5 also show that candidates who sought office in SMD places consistently scored lower on this factor, significantly so when we introduced controls for opposition, election outcome (candidate quality), and size of the jurisdiction. Candidates seeking office in SMD races thus not only spend less on their elections but do less in their campaigns as measured by factor 1. In other words, they may do fewer of the activities that can be seen as essential for disseminating information and generating interest in the local contest: speaking publicly, meeting reporters, mailing brochures, and printing and running political advertisements.[6]

Election System and Group-Based Campaign Assistance

Another potential aspect of a healthy local polity is the active involvement of groups that draw citizens into electoral politics. In table 5.1 we demonstrated a significant relationship between election system and a candidate's perception that organized groups work to mobilize voters.[7] However, as much as this might reveal something about CV campaigns, it does not tell us what else the groups do for candidates that might be affected by election rules. Given the increased incentives for campaign activity in CV (vs. SMD) and the findings from this chapter, we expected that the political activity of local groups on behalf of candidates would be greater in CV places than in plurality at-large places and that activity in SMD would be less frequent.

To test for this, we created a dichotomous variable that represented whether groups conducted any other activities on behalf of the candidate. In addition to the question about voter mobilization efforts, candidates were asked to check items from a list of twenty other activities that groups might have engaged in on their behalf. Since over 80 percent of candidates indicated that they had received no campaign help from organized groups, there was not enough variance in responses to create a useful additive index or to conduct a factor analysis. Thus, we created a variable that equaled one if groups assisted the candidates with one or more of the listed twenty activities and zero if otherwise. The most frequently cited activities that groups conducted on behalf of candidates (other than

TABLE 5.6. Estimations of Group-Based Campaign Activity (Dependent Variable = Group Campaigned on Behalf of Candidate)

Variables	Model 1	Model 2	Model 3	Model 4	Model 5
CV place	–.415	–.880	–1.32	–1.56+	–1.13
	(.705)	(.733)	(.854)	(.836)	(.737)
SMD place	—	–1.48+	–1.49+	–2.03*	–1.39
		(.910)	(.908)	(1.07)	(.962)
Minority candidate	1.33*	1.48*	1.12	2.19**	1.64*
	(.686)	(.701)	(.772)	(.844)	(.723)
Small place	–1.83**	–2.17**	–2.26**	–1.97**	–1.87**
	(.659)	(.704)	(.734)	(.744)	(.730)
Winner	—	—	–.014	—	—
			(.115)		
Incumbent	—	—	—	2.88*	—
				(1.22)	
Opposed	—	—	—	—	7.74
					(25.3)
Constant	–1.09	–0.23	0.37	–0.56	–15.5
	(1.29)	(1.38)	(1.46)	(1.42)	(50.6)
% correctly predicted	94.4	93.9	94.3	93.4	93.9
Model chi-square Improvement	10.72*	13.93**	13.78**	23.57**	17.68**
Number of cases	213	213	210	213	213

Note: Logistic regression estimates. Standard errors in parentheses. Dependent variable = 1 if group conducted one or more activities, 0 if otherwise.

** $p < .01$, two-tailed.
* = $p < .05$, two-tailed.
+ $p < .05$, one-tailed.

registration and mobilization) were posting signs, telephoning supporters, and walking precincts. We used logistic regression to estimate if candidates from CV or SMD places had more (or less) of this group-based campaign assistance in local elections. Once again, we used models that controlled for community size, minority status, election outcome, incumbency, and opposition. Results of the analysis of the variable created from the list of group-based assistance are reported in table 5.6.

In contrast to results of our estimations of the candidate's personal activity (table 5.5), we found that CV election rules were not associated with group-based activity that extended beyond vote mobilization. If anything, CV candidates reported slightly less assistance from organized groups, although this effect was significant only when we controlled for incumbency. Thus, while CV candidates were more likely to report that groups had worked to register and mobilize voters, table 5.6 shows that they were no more likely than other candidates to report that political groups had helped them in other ways.

Table 5.6 also reports that local SMD elections might depress another element of campaign activity. In three of the four estimations, SMD candidates reported significantly less group-based assistance than plurality at-large candidates. Not surprisingly, we found that there was less campaign assistance by groups in local elections in small communities. Another interesting finding among our control variables suggests an avenue for further study and is thus worth commenting on. When we controlled for community size and candidate attributes, we found that minority candidates were significantly more likely to report campaign assistance on their behalf by groups. Further analysis (e.g., table 4.4) found that minorities were also more likely than whites to claim that groups had mobilized/registered voters for them and that they themselves had worked personally to do this.[8]

These results, along with our other findings, illustrate that there is an effect of minority status on campaigning that transcends election system effects. We found some evidence that minority candidates spend less (table 5.3) than white candidates and that they campaign differently (or less directly as individuals) than white candidates (table 5.5). When combined with results in table 5.6, this suggests that minority candidates may compensate for disadvantages in campaign spending by relying more on local political organizations that register and mobilize voters, as well as conduct other campaign activities for the candidate. Put differently, white candidates are more likely to campaign as individuals and spend more money on their contests than minority candidates. These effects are independent of the electoral system. There are, then, some limits to the impacts of institutions and electoral engineering.

Discussion and Conclusion

It has been noted that one chronic problem for the maintenance of local democratic politics is a consistently low level of public interest in and knowledge of local affairs and an associated low level of participation (Elkin 1987). It is likely that given the relatively low salience of many local issues and the "consensus" politics surrounding much of what local governments do (Peterson 1981; conversely, see Donovan 1995), institutional reforms can do little to stimulate greater interest in local affairs. Our results suggest that one reform that might lead to more active campaigns, at least in that they are *contested* and involve efforts to mobilize voters, may be the use of CV elections.

Many racially and ethnically heterogeneous communities still use at-large election rules that depress minority representation and may be faced with the task of changing their election rules. Such communities, with lines of political conflict drawn over racial and ethnic issues, often lack the political consensus that Peterson (1981) and others assume. Districting may appear an attractive alternative to an at-large system, since it does incorporate minorities into local elected boards and councils. The price of incorporation, however, may be election rules that discourage certain campaign activities and in particular may well reduce the number of candidates competing and hence the choices open to voters.

CV could also prove attractive to these places due to its ability to incorporate minorities into elected bodies. But there are other aspects of CV that might prove attractive to communities contemplating a switch away from standard at-large elections. While candidates spend less in SMD races than candidates contesting offices in other places, SMD elections also involve less activity by organized groups. Furthermore, compared to candidates seeking CV seats, candidates seeking office in SMD places use less of what we see as a direct, active style of campaigning. These data suggest that candidates must work a bit harder to win and retain seats under CV than districting. In short, compared to SMD, CV probably increases electoral competitiveness. If competitive elections are important, if they encourage interest in politics and instill legitimacy in elected bodies, these should be seen as important differences.

Districting, in theory, produces representation that is grounded in a relatively small geographic area, allowing a representative to have links with constituents that allow him or her to better represent their interests.[9] If, however, contested elections and the associated information flow associated with them are valuable in and of themselves, the benefits of SMD elections may be outweighed by trade-offs that detract from the quality of political competition in a community.

▪ 6 ▪

Voter Response to Campaigns and New Election Rules

The discussion thus far has largely centered on how electoral rules affect the activity and behavior of parties and candidates. In this chapter and the next we turn our attention to how citizens might respond to elite attempts to solve vote coordination problems and mobilize voters.

Ordinal electoral systems such as cumulative voting (CV), the alternative vote (AV), mixed-member proportional (MMP) systems, and the single transferable vote (STV) all permit the expression of more preferences than other types of electoral system. Under CV, voters can decide how to apportion a variable number of votes across a number of candidates that they select. Under AV and STV, voters can rank-order a number of candidates, and with MMP, they can support a candidate of one party with their district (electorate) vote and decide if another party will get their party-list vote. These preferential (or ordinal) systems give citizens the ability to tailor their voting more precisely, using the flexibility of the ballot to come up with many different ways of expressing their preferences for representation. Richness in preference expression comes at the cost of increased complexity of the task facing voters.

Doubts about citizens' ability to deal with such complexity have been one of the most common critiques of the class of ordinal electoral systems as a whole[1] as well as of CV specifically (Dunn and Gove 1972; Dunn 1972; Everson et al. 1982; Still 1984). In chapter 3, for example, we drew attention to Rae's comment about CV systems that reflected such concerns: "One would expect that the rather complex cognitive arrangements necessary for ordinal voting are likely to be quite rare" (Rae 1971, 128).[2] Since ordinal systems require a great deal of coordination among voters, especially if proportionality of outcomes is a concern, an important issue to be addressed is the empirical one of whether real-world voters can deal with the complexities of systems such as CV.

Voting under Complex Electoral Systems

Most of the time, single-member districting (SMD) and other majoritarian plans do not invoke the need for voters to think very much beyond voting a sincere expression of a single preference.[3] Party-list proportional representation (PR) typically offers even fewer opportunities to vote tactically. While in principle any election that involves the choice between more than two candidates holds open the possibility (or the need) for strategic voting, in practice the scope for such behavior often remains limited. It is not surprising, then, that in terms of a generic model of voting behavior, strategic issues have formed a relatively small part of the literature. But these issues would seem to form a bigger part of voting behavior under ordinal electoral rules where candidates and parties need voters to cast their ballots in quite specific ways. Here, the question of whether voters act strategically is doubly important, since proportional representation may not be possible unless voters respond to elite instructions for strategic voting. In fact, a British Royal Commission on electoral system reform dismissed CV because it relied on this kind of voter response, arguing that "its successful operation requires the implicit obedience of the elector to the directions of the party manager. A system which depends for its efficiency on such a requirement as this stands self condemned" (Royal Commission 1910, 13).

As we demonstrated in chapters 3 and 4, if a group's supporters cannot become aware of and responsive to vote dispersion strategies, the group's representation may be diluted. As we saw, candidates may be able to solve vote management and nomination puzzles, but what about voters? After all, no matter how astute candidates and parties may be, their vote coordination strategies will matter little if voters ignore them. If voters cannot respond, we cannot expect alternative systems such as CV to provide minority groups with descriptive representation. Because of the nonpartisan nature of local elections, one of the main means of organizing the vote is missing. Absence of the important coordinating device of party forces candidates and their supporting organizations to assume this role, raising a further question: Can voters respond to the strategic demands of CV without strong local party organizations?

Citizen Response to Complex Rules: Cumulative Voting in the United States

Concern about citizen response to CV has been evident in studies of jurisdictions adopting CV. Public education campaigns, for example, were conducted in Chilton County, Alabama (Pildes and Donoghue 1995, 268–71), Alamogordo, New Mexico (Cole, Taebel, and Engstrom 1990), and other communities (Engstrom and Barrilleaux 1991). These efforts included public meetings and newspaper advertisements crafted to educate citizens about how their votes could be distributed in CV. Key public figures associated with the adoption of CV also took it upon themselves to educate citizens about the voting system (Pildes and Donoghue 1995, 270). Since U.S. voters had no experience with preferential or ordinal voting, there were fears that voters would not understand that they could plump multiple votes on a single candidate or spread support across multiple candidates.

Richard Barnett, a Chicago political activist experienced with CV campaigns in Illinois, is one writer who challenges fears that CV can prove too confusing to citizens. According to Barnett, "For poor urban areas, like the West Side, CV you could explain to people, because folks understand numbers" (Center for Voting and Democracy [CVD] Transcript 1999). Or as another activist from Chicago noted of voter response to CV, "They could figure it out. You could quickly explain to them, 'Look, if you give all your votes to such-and-such a candidate, to Paul Simon, we can beat the machine.' They would understand that" (CVD Transcript 1999).

Many of the early empirical studies of CV in the United States, then, were motivated by questions of voter comprehension of CV. A series of papers discussing the results of exit polls conducted in early CV elections have convincingly demonstrated that white voters and minority voters readily understand this system. Ninety-five percent of Alamogordo voters interviewed in that city's first CV election reported that they knew they could "plump," and over 86 percent responded that the system was no more complicated than others (Cole, Taebel, and Engstrom 1990, 194). Brischetto (1995) found similar levels of voter comprehension in his exit surveys of sixteen Texas CV communities contesting elections in 1995. More than nine out of ten voters in his exit polls—Latinos, blacks, and whites alike—reported that they knew they could plump all of their votes on a single candidate (Brischetto 1995, 352). Here we can provide some examples of voter understanding by using survey data from an exit poll conducted by Richard Engstrom and Charles Barrilleaux during the first CV school board election held in Sisseton, South Dakota. Engstrom and Barrilleaux administered surveys to nearly all 808 voters in the election, and 261 completed their survey.[4]

Under at-large voting, only one of twenty-three Native American candidates had been elected to the board since 1977 (Engstrom and Barrilleaux 1991). With the first three-seat CV election, the minority group (Native Americans) commanded a great enough share of the jurisdiction's population (34 percent) that they could expect to win one seat via CV under favorable circumstances. Using the formula from chapter 2, we see that the threshold of exclusion in a three-seat CV race is 25 percent. That is, if one of the group's candidates can secure at least 25 percent of the vote, the group cannot be excluded from representation. For Native Americans in Sisseton, being this close to the threshold meant that representation was possible only if turnout was close to that of whites (assuming little

TABLE 6.1. Voter Knowledge of CV Strategies, Sisseton, South Dakota

Knew could plump?	Not Native American	Native American	Total
Yes	100 (89%)	127 (90%)	227 (90%)
No	12 (11%)	14 (10%)	26 (10%)
Total	112 (100%)	141 (100%)	253 (100%)

Source: Exit poll conducted by Engstrom and Barrilleaux (1991).

TABLE 6.2. Voter Evaluations of CV Difficulty, Sisseton, South Dakota

Believed election system harder than others?	Not Native American	Native American	Total
Yes	17 (15%)	15 (11%)	32 (13%)
No	95 (85%)	126 (89%)	221 (87%)
Total	112	141	253

Source: Exit poll conducted by Engstrom and Barrilleaux (1991).

crossover voting) and/or if nearly all Native American voters plumped their votes on the same candidate. One Native American sought a seat in the election.[5]

It is clear from the evidence of table 6.1 that most Sisseton voters knew that CV provided them the opportunity to plump their votes. This level of this knowledge for minority voters is particularly important—90 percent of Native Americans surveyed in Sisseton claimed to be aware they could plump. This demonstrates these voters had sufficient understanding of the key strategic aspect of CV that would allow them to win a seat. Moreover, as table 6.2 shows, the overwhelming majority of voters (roughly 88 percent of the total sample) did not believe the system was harder to understand "compared to other local elections in which you have voted." Furthermore, Native American voters did not find the system especially burdensome and did understand the workings of the system.

Table 6.3 breaks down these data in another way by presenting information on the voters' turnout history. Those who "almost always" voted in local elections were slightly (but not significantly) more likely to claim that CV was harder to understand than other elections. Occasional and new voters, conversely, were slightly less likely to say CV was harder. Aside from the observation that this could simply be a reflection of the hold that custom has on voting habits, we can note that Anglo voters were ones who turned out more regularly. CV is likely to generate some opposition from white elites and voters who realize that it can break white monopoly control of local councils (Cole, Taebel, and

TABLE 6.3. New Voters' Evaluations of CV Difficulty, Sisseton, South Dakota

	Do You Usually Vote in School Board Elections?			
	Almost Always	Occasionally	Never	Total
Evaluation of CV:				
Found CV harder	23 (14%)	4 (8%)	4 (11%)	31 (12%)
Did not find CV harder	143 (86%)	44 (92%)	32 (88.9%)	219 (88%)
Total	166 (100%)	48 (100%)	36 (11.1)	250 (100%)

Source: Exit poll conducted by Engstrom and Barrilleaux (1991).

Engstrom 1990, 195). The evidence of tables 6.1, 6.2, and 6.3, then, demonstrates that even new voters, particularly minority voters, readily understand CV.

All of this suggests that voters understand what they *may* do in a CV election. But do they actually respond to strategic appeals? Did they even receive any such appeals? In some situations the incentive for candidates to ask voters to plump can be particularly strong. If a group has only one candidate (as a result of having a low minority vote share), we should expect the candidate's campaign activities to include calls for vote plumping. The incentive stems from the fact that, if a candidate's base of support is limited to a minority group and the group is at or near the threshold of exclusion, no candidate of the group can win unless supporters plump votes. Although all candidates may desire that supporters plump, minority candidates (and voters) are far more heavily dependent upon plumping. Campaigns of minority candidates may thus be expected to make more frequent use of requests for vote plumping from supporters.

Table 6.4 speaks to the question of whether voters receive party—or in this case group and candidate—vote coordination strategies. These data are limited to survey respondents who reported their voting behavior in the exit poll (211 of 261). Although only 15 percent of voters reported being contacted by a campaign, cross-tabulations of these data demonstrate that campaign contacts were virtually limited to Native American voters. Twenty-four percent reported being contacted and asked to give all of their votes to the Native American candidate, David Selvage, while only 4 percent of white voters reported campaign contacts.

It is one thing for minority voters to report that they receive the campaign's message to vote strategically and quite another for them to respond to these

TABLE 6.4. Voter Reports of Campaign Contacts and Requests for Plumping, by Racial Group of Voter

	Race of Voter		
Contacts?	**White**	**Native American**	**Total**
Contacted by campaign and asked to plump	4 (4.4%)	29 (23.9)	33 (15.6%)
Not contacted, not asked to plump	86 (95.6%)	92 (76.1)	178 (84.4%)
Total	90 (100%)	121 (100%)	211 (100%)

Note: Chi-square = 14.93, $p < .01$.
Source: Exit poll conducted by Engstrom and Barrilleaux (1991).

messages. Evidence of plumping in favor of the minority candidates in Sisseton and other CV communities would suggest that minority voters receive and respond to candidate vote coordination strategies. Table 6.5a illustrates that in the Sisseton election, 88 percent of the vote base of Selvage (the Native American candidate) was from plumped votes. This figure stands in stark contrast to the vote base of the remaining candidates and, as the earlier data in table 6.1 indicated, is not attributable to different levels of knowledge about the system between Native American and other voters. It is not the case, for example, that only Native Americans knew they could plump. They knew they could plump, they received campaign information requesting them to plump, and many did in fact plump.

The result was that Selvage was elected, finishing first place in a race for three seats and collecting 31 percent of all votes (Engstrom and Barrilleaux 1991, 390). The Sisseton exit polls identified that Selvage received 90 percent of his support from Native Americans—93 percent of whom reported plumping their votes. Selvage also received 90 percent of all Native American votes recorded in the exit poll. In contrast, the second-, third-, and fourth-place (white) finishers received 25 percent, 16 percent, and 15 percent of white votes respectively. Only 32 percent of white voters reported plumping all three of their votes on a single candidate, with another 22 percent reporting that they gave one candidate two votes. Election results and survey data in table 6.5a suggest that white candidates and voters were unable or unwilling to engage in the vote dispersion coordination efforts that we found with majority groups in Victorian England. Since only one Native American candidate ran, and since Native American voters were mobilized and responded to call for plumping, Selvage could capture more votes and cross the threshold of exclusion. In this instance,

TABLE 6.5. Plumping in Local CV Elections in the United States: Percentage of Minority Candidate's Votes Received by Type of Vote

a. Sisseton, South Dakota School Board, 1991

Candidate	% from Voters Casting *n* Votes			% Vote for Cand.
	1	2	3	
Selvage	7%	5%	88%	31.7%
Five others	70%	10%	20%	63.3%

b. Alamogordo, New Mexico, City Council, 1987, Three Seats Elected

Candidate	% from Voters Casting *n* Votes			% Vote for Cand.
	1	2	3	
Downs	33%	21%	46%	22.4%
Riordan	43%	23%	34%	19.5%
Moncada	24%	14%	61%	19.3%
Carrol	51%	19%	29%	16.7%
Seamans	65%	17%	42%	8.8%
Three others	43%	12%	45%	13.3%

c. Peoria, Illinois, City Council, Five Seats Elected

Candidate	% from Voters Casting *n* Votes					% Vote for Cand.
	1	1.25	1.67	2.5	5	
Unes	12%	8%	18%	30%	33%	20.7%
Spears	14%	7%	16%	25%	38%	12.7%
Gibson	19%	11%	23%	26%	22%	12.2%
Ledoux	16%	10%	21%	26%	26%	11.4%
Glover	18%	9%	19%	24%	30%	11.1%
Allen	12%	7%	13%	26%	41%	7.7%
OBrien	22%	10%	19%	21%	28%	7.3%
Banks	9%	6%	13%	23%	49%	7.2%
Casper	24%	10%	15%	17%	34%	5.0%
Johnson	12%	8%	12%	24%	43%	4.8%

Note: Others include white candidates only. Minority candidates and candidates' votes received as "plumps" in shaded area.

Sources: Sisseton, Exit poll by Engstrom and Barrilleaux (1991); Alamogordo, Exit poll by Taebel, Engstrom, and Cole (1999, 28); Peoria, Board of Elections (Aspin 1996).

white voters could deny the Native American candidate a seat *only* if they had been organized to "outmobilize" Native American voters and coordinate on a strategy for dispersing votes across three specific candidates. This case suggests that the strategic demands for vote coordination created by CV election systems might be more easily met by a minority organizing for plumping than by majorities who need to organize for voter dispersion. Indeed, all of the exit polls from New Mexico, South Dakota, and Texas, as well as our surveys of candidates running under CV, demonstrate that minority voters are less likely than whites to claim that the system is difficult to understand or that it is a bad election system.[6]

The types of votes that minority candidates received in other CV elections are displayed in tables 6.5b and 6.5c. Chapter 4 noted the appeal from Inez Moncada's campaign advertisements requesting voters to give her all three of their votes in Alamogordo, New Mexico's 1987 three-seat council election. It would seem that her appeals were effective. Sixty-one percent of her votes came from voters who gave her all three of their votes. The comparable level of plumping for other (nonminority) candidates in Alamogordo was much less. There is evidence, furthermore, that minority voters were most likely to plump in Alamogordo, as in Sisseton. Exit polls in that community found that Moncada received votes from 73 percent of Latino voters, 68 percent of whom reported they plumped (another 11 percent gave two of three votes to Moncada). This compared to 39 percent of white voters who plumped—with another 29 percent giving two of three votes to one candidate (Cole, Taebel, and Engstrom 1990, 195). Exit polls illustrate that Moncada placed fourth in the number of voters supporting her but that plumping from Latinos led her to collect enough total votes to place third (Engstrom, Taebel, and Cole 1989, 491). Since Latinos constituted 24 percent of the voting-age population in Alamogordo, and since the threshold of exclusion in a three-seat race is 25 percent, effective voting strategy (plumping) among Latinos was essential for Moncada's election. Yet unlike Selvage's election in Sisseton, Moncada also drew support from Anglos. Twenty-two percent of Anglo voters supported Moncada, most giving her one of their votes (Cole, Taebel, and Engstrom 1990, 197).

Exit polls in Texas conducted by Brischetto and Engstrom (1997) produced similar results. Looking at fifteen communities having CV elections in 1995, they found that 66 percent of Latino voters plumped for a single candidate, with 82 percent of Latinos plumping for a Latino candidate. Only 37 percent of Anglo voters reported plumping in Texas (Brischetto and Engstrom 1997, 979).

Results of the first (1991) CV city council election in Peoria, Illinois, show a somewhat different pattern of plumping for minority candidates. In a city where African Americans constituted 21 percent of the voting-age population, the five-seat CV contest produced a threshold for exclusion of 16.7 percent. Four African

American candidates survived the primary, presenting a potential vote dilution problem. If voting in Peoria were highly polarized along racial lines, we would expect that a single black candidate would have been able to win if minority voters plumped. Racially polarized voting could have also prevented minority representation if African American votes were dispersed across candidates who drew no support from white voters. In the end, black candidates received a total of 31 percent of votes, suggesting either that black voters turned out at a higher rate than whites or that black candidates received support from black and white voters. Given the low vote total for the least-supported winning candidate (11.1 percent), a vote coordination strategy that concentrated all support for black candidates on two individuals could have produced an "extra" African American member of the council.

Whatever the hypothetical possibilities may have been, the distribution of votes received by the single African American who was elected (Ledoux) illustrates at least two things. First, minority candidates need not always rely heavily on plumping to win under CV. The pattern of support for Ledoux from different vote types looks quite similar to that for white candidates shown in table 6.5. Ledoux received only 26 percent of support in plumped votes. Second, minority candidates who are reasonably successful at attracting plumped votes are not assured of winning, particularly if they are competing for plumps with other minority candidates.

There is a mechanical factor that may affect the ability for candidates to attract concentrated votes in Peoria. Peoria's CV ballot system does not allow an unequal concentration of votes across two or more candidates. In most CV systems used in the United States, voters plump by voting with individual marks for each vote they cast. If elections are held for three seats, three boxes are located at each candidate's name. This gives voters the discretion to give two votes to one candidate and one to another (as in Alamogordo and Sisseton). Chilton County, Alabama, and Guin, Alabama, elect seven seats, so voters can give one candidate six votes and another a single vote, and so forth. But Peoria's ballot lists only one box next to each candidate, and marking successive candidates *dilutes* the vote across each name marked. Machines are programmed to read a single mark as a plump. If a voter marks next to two candidates, the machine reads the vote as 2.5 voters per candidate, three marks are read as 1.67 votes per candidate, and so on. Thus, if a voter sends *any* support to a second candidate, she dilutes her votes equally across both.

Conclusion: Voter Response to Mobilization Efforts

Our examination of voter behavior in U.S. local CV elections demonstrates that in rural, nonpartisan settings such as Sisseton, minority candidates appear able to effectively translate some level of vote coordination strategies to their

TABLE 6.6. Response to Mobilizing Effects of CV Election, Sisseton, South Dakota

Do You Usually Vote in School Board Elections	Not Native American	Native American	Total
Almost always	93 (85%)	78 (54%)	171 (67%)
Occasionally	13 (11%)	35 (24%)	48 (19%)
Never	4 (4%)	32 (22%)	36 (14%)
Total	110 (100%)	145 (100%)	255 (100%)

Source: Exit poll conducted by Engstrom and Barrilleaux (1991).

electoral base, and voters appear to respond to the need to vote strategically and plump for a particular minority candidate. Effective communication of plumping strategies, moreover, can be critically important for a minority group seeking representation in a jurisdiction where the group is near the threshold of exclusion. U.S. candidates and voters, not unlike their Australian counterparts, appear able to respond to the strategic demands of CV elections.

This examination of voter response to complex electoral settings would not be complete without some consideration of how voters might be mobilized in CV elections. In previous chapters, we presented the idea that by creating new opportunities for representation, CV might mobilize voters from groups who were excluded from representation under plurality election rule (Amy 1993, 279). We also demonstrated that CV candidates reported groups working in their communities to mobilize and register new voters (chapter 5). The issue is critical. Brischetto and Engstrom (1997) have established empirically that minority candidates have little chance of being elected if their participation levels fall below the threshold of exclusion in a jurisdiction. In other words, it seems that minority candidates are well capable of transmitting the necessary instructions for strategic behavior. We have suggested here that the simplicity of asking for plumping may make vote coordination easier for minorities than the vote dispersion coordination that a majority group has to engage in to maximize seats. Yet solving these strategic voting issues is perhaps all for naught if a minority group cannot mobilize its supporters.

Exit poll data from Sisseton suggest that the voter mobilization efforts associated with CV campaigns (see chapters 4 and 5) may pay dividends for minority groups. Table 6.6 presents evidence suggesting that the Sisseton CV election and its associated campaign activity may have drawn new minority voters to the polls. Nearly half of Native American respondents claimed to be rare or occasional voters (24 percent and 22 percent, respectively), while only 15 percent of white voters fell into either category. This latter finding is consistent with our observations about campaign activity. Since turnout is required to translate the strategic votes of minority voters into representation, we will examine the aggregate consequences of CV elections for turnout in the next chapter.

· 7 ·

Alternative Electoral Rules and Voter Mobilization

Our discussion of the strategic demands made by ordinal electoral systems assumed that minority and majority voters participate in elections at equal rates. While this assumption simplified the presentation of those strategic demands, it masked an important qualification. If voters from one group turn out at lower levels than another, efficient coordination of candidate nominations and supporters' voting behavior may all be for naught. The threshold of exclusion, for example, is often discussed in terms of a group's share of a jurisdiction's *population.* This can create the false impression that a group is assured of representation if it is well organized and larger than the threshold. But the actual allocation of seats is based not on population but on the share of the *vote.* Even perfect plumping on a single candidate will translate into seats only if the group's voters show up at the polls; especially if the underlying voting-age population of the group is close to the threshold of exclusion. We can recast this problem in more positive terms: cumulative voting (CV) and limited voting (LV) systems have built-in incentives for elites to mobilize potential voters as fully as possible.

Earlier, we noted that electoral rules create incentives affecting how elites and voters interact and behave. We suggest here that winner-take-all at-large plans, by shutting minorities out from representation and thereby eliminating a major source of electoral competition, reduce the incentives elites have to mobilize voters. Single-member districts (SMDs) will have similar effects. To the extent that districting plans produce relatively homogeneous districts, within-district minorities (e.g., Anglos within a majority black district) may have little incentive to turn out, and candidates may have little incentive to mobilize them.

Campaign activity by candidates is an important antecedent to voter turnout, and previously we showed some differences in campaign activity of candidates between simple-plurality elections (either single member or at large) and CV elections. We established that CV election campaigns are different from plurality campaigns in subtle but important ways. We found, for example, that CV candidates were more likely than plurality candidates to report that groups were working to mobilize and register voters in their community (chapters 4 and 5). Compared to plurality candidates, moreover, CV candidates spent more money on their campaigns and were more likely to use a campaign style that relied upon canvassing and contacting voters (chapter 5). Exit polls from Sisseton (chapter 6) also illustrate that a CV contest can mobilize minority voters who claim to have rarely participated in local elections. In this chapter, we assess the behavioral consequences of these factors in terms of how they may produce higher levels of voter participation in places using CV elections.

Do Institutions Matter? Turnout in Comparative Perspective

The idea that electoral institutions can promote turnout is not especially novel. A series of cross-national studies of voter participation by Powell (1986), Jackman and Miller (1995), and others (Blais and Carty 1990; Blais and Dobrzynska 1998) argue that institutional factors such as election rules—rather than just individual demographic traits—are key determinants of variations in turnout. A complementary category of institutional explanations of U.S. voter turnout stresses institutional forces. Rusk (1970) identified that Australian ballots reduced turnout in the United States. Burnham (1970, 93–94) noted that "depoliticizing and antipartisan" changes in state election rules (affecting primaries, apportionment, third-party ballot access, and off-year state election scheduling) probably resulted in a new, lower equilibrium level of participation. Nonpartisan elections and "off-year" scheduling also reduce participation in local elections (Alford and Lee 1968). Jackson, Brown, and Wright (1998); Nagler (1991); Caldeira, Patterson, and Markko (1985); Rosenstone and Wolfinger (1978); and others have demonstrated the barriers that registration laws place on voting. Patterson and Caldeira (1983) also emphasized the mobilizing role of partisan campaigns, but Rosenstone and Hansen (1993) identified the weakening effects that contemporary party organizations have on mobilizing voters. Hill and Leighley (1993) found that interparty competitiveness is associated with higher turnout, but not party organization. Structural features such as the closeness or competitiveness of House races (Cox and Munger 1989) and adverse economic conditions (Rosenstone 1982) have also been shown to affect levels of participation.

Single-nation studies of individual voter decisions are often embedded within a specific institutional context and must therefore stress individual demographic and attitudinal factors (e.g., education) as the primary determinants of the decision to turn out and vote. In explaining a decline in U.S. national turnout since 1960, Abramson and Aldrich (1982) suggested, for example, that voters had lower levels of political efficacy than in decades past (also see Verba and Nie 1972). Shaffer (1981) noted the role these forces play and added that the potential electorate became younger and less informed by 1980. Wolfinger and Rosenstone (1980) gave particular weight to education (also see Verba, Nie, and Kim 1978; Verba and Nie 1972; Campbell et al. 1960), while Leighley and Nagler (1992) demonstrated that although the effects of some individual forces changed over time, education remained the primary determinant of voting.

Once we change focus and compare across political systems, however, the explanations shift from focusing on individual-level factors to emphasizing the effects of institutional context. Wolfinger and Rosenstone (1980), for example, argued that state registration laws in the United States serve as an important explanation of variation in voter participation. Jackman (1987) pointed to the importance of proportionality of the electoral system, as well as other constitutional factors such as whether the legislature is unicameral or not. Blais and Carty (1990) showed that when alternative explanations are controlled for in a multivariate model, proportional representation (PR) systems still are associated with higher levels of voter participation. They were silent, however, on the exact mechanism by which PR enhances turnout, leading Amy (1993) to offer his own list of possible explanations—including the adverse effect of plurality rules on attitudes that cause citizens to see any value in voting.

One probable attitudinal disincentive for most voters in SMD or plurality at-large jurisdictions is that they waste votes (Lijphart 1994; Swain 1993; Thernstrom 1987; Still 1984). Districts are often drawn to ensure that a candidate from a given party will be victorious; this habit can also be found in nonpartisan municipal races that feature polarized racial voting. The wasted votes are defined as all of those for the losing side (votes that were not translated into representation) and those from the winning side in excess of the minimum required for election (Lijphart 1994; Still 1984). Amy argued that voters on both the losing and winning sides in noncompetitive districts quickly realize the futility of voting (see also Guinier 1994, 94–97). The votes, especially those of the losing candidate, are not translated into representation and have no chance to turn the tide in either one direction or another. If a voter senses that his or her vote, with certainty, will not elect a representative, then there is no tangible return on the investment required in the act of voting. The voter has little remaining motivation to vote and consequently fails to do so.

The Stimulative Effects of PR and Semi-PR Rules on Turnout

PR and, to a lesser extent, semi-PR systems operate, at least in theory, to promote turnout both through their effect on voters and through their effect on candidates. Candidate campaigning activity should be higher under PR, and this should, in turn, affect turnout. Douglas Amy (1993), for example, argued that PR systems ought to feature more effort by parties in mobilizing voters, and that this mobilization effort will result in increased voter participation in the election. The mobilization effort is more likely to feature in PR systems because such systems feature fewer safe seats, and parties have a strong incentive to mobilize in every district where they have measurable support. Any increase in that support at the ballot box will translate into additional seats at a much higher rate than in a system based entirely on SMDs.

Electoral systems can also shape candidates' decision to enter the race at all by shaping their expectations of the outcome: if candidates believe they cannot win, they are unlikely to compete or spend a great deal of effort competing. But a reduced number of candidates is likely to mean a reduced number of issues and interests being expressed by candidates. In multimember districts (MMDs), the greater the district magnitude (the number of seats in the district), the lower the minimum threshold for representation (Lijphart 1994), and with a lower threshold of representation we ought to see more candidates representing a greater range of interests.[1] Such a picture contrasts with that found in SMDs, where the potential for a safe seat will reduce competitiveness. A district specifically drawn to elect a black candidate, for example, may easily dampen competition. In such a setting, quality challengers may well decide not to run and waste their time, especially if they are not of the same ethnicity as the within-district majority. Second, as discussed above, voters who would otherwise vote for such a challenger lack incentive to turn out, considering the predetermined nature of the election. In short, the same kinds of arguments that are brought to bear in discussions of minority voters in society at large will also apply to within-district minorities. And the same kind of arguments about how voter expectations of closeness in result affect turnout (a close race implying higher turnout, a not very close race depressing turnout) will also hold at the district level when the districts are drawn in such a way as to ensure certain kinds of results.

In principle, systems such as CV feature MMDs that can allow multiple issue-oriented candidacies to exist by shaping expectations of winning. The larger variety of ways to stack up electoral coalitions under ordinal systems such as CV offers candidates several different ways to win. A potentially strong candidate who lacks incentive to run in a plurality SMD has incentive under an MMD to try and piece together an issue-based (or ethnic- or neighborhood-based) coalition, thus encouraging candidacy.

More choices, and clearer choices, that result from candidate decisions to enter and compete are two reasons why PR systems increase participation rates for voters. With more choices, chances are that more voters will have a candidate to vote for who is in close proximity to their own views. Amy (1993) argued that when one votes for a candidate close to one's own views, voting is a more "satisfying experience" and more people are likely to partake in voting.

Duverger (1954) illustrated that electoral systems based on SMDs tend to reward candidates with centrist positions. Amy, drawing on Downs (1957), argued that this may have a perverting effect on turnout rates. When candidate positions are in close proximity, information distinguishing them (and thus clarifying the choice for a voter) is harder to come by and more difficult to interpret.[2] This increases uncertainty in voters, thus reducing the likelihood that a person will cast a vote. Amy argued that PR systems mitigate the forces that drive candidates toward the median voter. Indeed, PR—and by extension, semi-PR—plans encourage candidates to stake out their own distinct "turf" on a given issue or policy (see also Cox 1997 for a discussion of this point and of Cox's earlier formal results on the topic). With greater variety in candidates' issue positions as strategies as well as greater numbers of candidates, voters may well be given greater incentive to turn out and vote.

Empirically then, we expect CV elections to feature stronger, opposing candidacies. Since parties or slating groups have more incentive to mobilize supporters, these stronger candidacies should result in more competitive elections with higher voter turnout.

Comparing Turnout in CV/LV and Plurality U.S. Local Elections

While cross-national empirical studies typically find that plurality rules depress turnout, these findings are not beyond question. The relatively small number of countries considered in such studies means that there are usually too few degrees of freedom to control for the place-specific factors that might covary with institutional factors. For example, electoral system variables in the Powell and Jackman studies distinguish between two groups of cases that have different levels of turnout. But each group also has distinct historical, social, or cultural traits that could affect participation. This is particularly problematic because one explanation of participation is that nations may have distinctive "political cultures" that affect their citizens' "subjective orientation to politics" (Verba 1965, 513). This might cause high (or low) turnout regardless of election rules among countries with shared historical backgrounds. Given that the presumed institutional effect identified in cross-national studies is subject to these doubts, it may be the case that changing the electoral system does not boost turnout. The dynamic effect of increasing turnout being associated with changing the electoral rules is inferred from the cross-sectional results, which are, as we noted, quite difficult to disentangle from other possible causes.

Although these reservations relating to the empirical basis of the finding that links electoral system and turnout using cross-national data are quite serious, our own data set allows a more robust test of electoral system effects. As noted at the outset of this book, much of our analysis is based on data collected from a set of communities that were selected for study because they were similar on many traits but varied in their election rules. This allowed us to assess the effect of election systems on turnout by examining variation in rules across places where contextual and cultural factors were, for the most part, held constant by our research design. Hence we could avoid one of the main critiques of the cross-national studies. We did this by combining a quasi-experimental case selection method with both cross-sectional and longitudinal statistical analysis where we compared U.S. communities using "semiproportional" systems to those using plurality rules.

Data on turnout in local elections were requested from the largest jurisdictions in the United States that currently employ either CV or LV. Although approximately 100 jurisdictions have used CV, a number of them are very small towns. We sought turnout data from only forty-five of those CV places having a 1990 population over 1,000 persons. Nearly every place that has adopted CV or LV has done so in the context of conflict over limited (or nonexistent) representation of African Americans and Latinos, and all these places have sizable minority populations. Of these forty-five places, we received turnout data from twenty-eight (a 62 percent response rate).

For comparison, turnout data were also obtained from a set of communities using plurality elections. The second set of cases was carefully selected so that each plurality jurisdiction closely matched a specific CV place in terms of key geographic and social characteristics. The 1990 U.S. Census was used for this purpose, allowing us to identify community-level measures of race and ethnicity, population size, percentage of residents having a high school degree, and median income. Each jurisdiction using CV was matched with a plurality jurisdiction of similar size having similar levels of median income, high school graduates, and minority (nonwhite) population. For example, we obtained turnout data for several elections from the city of Alamogordo, New Mexico (1990 pop. 27,595; 25 percent Latino, 6 percent African American; median income $24,579), which used CV from 1987 to 1994. These cases were matched with turnout data from the city of Clovis, New Mexico (1990 pop. 30,954; 36 percent Latino, 7 percent African American; median income $21,222), and turnout data for various years were obtained from local officials in that community. Likewise, the plurality jurisdiction matched with the CV city of Peoria, Illinois (1990 pop. 113,504; 21 percent African American; median income $26,074) was Rockford, Illinois (1990 pop. 139,426; 16 percent African American; median income $28,282). In the end, we obtained turnout data for twenty-one of the twenty-eight plurality jurisdictions matched with the CV/LV places from which we received data.

These matched cases thus supplied a control group with major demographic factors highly similar to those found in the CV places, yet the control places employed different electoral systems (always plurality elections). Each control city was located in the same state and generally in the same county as the "experimental" CV city it was matched with. If CV school districts or counties were being matched with control cases, then similar jurisdictions were identified in close proximity to the experimental place. Using this design of keeping most factors other than election system constant across all experimental and control cases, we were able to compare CV places with plurality places that had similar conditions. Furthermore, nearly all of these jurisdictions scheduled local elections independently of state and federal races, so other contests that might mobilize voters were also held constant.[3]

Between 1997 and 1999, city and county clerks and school district offices in the experimental and control jurisdictions were surveyed for voter turnout data in recent elections. Officials in CV places were also asked to supply data from their elections held under CV or LV and from the final three elections held under plurality at-large systems. This allowed us to conduct a longitudinal analysis of change in turnout within the set of "experimental" communities, in addition to the cross-sectional analysis of differences in turnout between the experimental (CV) cases and the control (plurality) cases. Overall, forty-nine different jurisdictions (twenty-eight CV and twenty-one plurality) supplied turnout data on 216 elections.[4] The majority of these jurisdictions staggered the election of seats, with elections for three or four seats held annually or every two years in many places.

A smaller number of places in Alabama and North Carolina adopted LV elections (one Texas community also used LV). Since the LV places were often very small towns, we were unable to contact officials in many of these places or their matched counterparts. Although we did obtain turnout data for twenty-eight LV elections from six jurisdictions, we were unable to generate sufficient data from matched communities for these places. This being the case, information about LV elections is omitted from the bulk of our analysis.

Table 7.1 reports mean turnout levels (our dependent variable) for four different groups of cases and also reports group means for the key independent variables used to match the control and experimental cases. Individual cases in each group represent a jurisdiction's election in a specific year.[5] Apart from slight variation in median income across the groups of cases, the jurisdictions in each group are nearly identical in terms of the average size of minority populations (37–38 percent) and average proportion of residents with a high school

TABLE 7.1. Descriptive Characteristics: All Cases, Controls, and Experimental Groups

Variable	All Elections	Continuous Plurality Elections (Controls)	Plurality Elections Prior to CV (Exp. Pre)	CV Elections after Switch from Plurality (Exp. Post)
Turnout %	19 (14)	17 (16)	18(12)	24 (14)
Minority %	38 (15)	38 (14)	37 (14)	38 (16)
High school education %	56 (10)	56 (09)	55 (10)	55 (11)
Median income	$19,753 ($3,869)	21,210 (3,910)	18,807 (3,308)	19,256 (3,988)
Total number of elections	216	72	74	70

Note: Main entries are means; standard deviations are in parentheses. Control groups: Places using plurality elections matched with demographic and geographic traits of CV places.
Experimental pre: Places using plurality contests prior to using new CV system.
Experimental post: CV places after switching from plurality.

T-tests were used to calculate the lowest margin between means that would be significantly different, using an alpha of .01.

education (55–56 percent). The table illustrates that across all types of elections in these places, turnout in local elections averaged 19 percent.

Our control group (plurality elections from the matched jurisdictions) included turnout results from 72 elections.[6] Since longer time series were obtained from places using CV, we had turnout data for more elections from CV places (74 from at-large elections before adopting CV, 70 from CV elections after). Turnout was expressed as a percentage of the voting-age population that cast a ballot in the given local election. Turnout figures were obtained from the relevant jurisdictions, while all other demographic variables used in this analysis were drawn from either the 1990 U.S. Census, or, in the case of school districts, the School District Data Book on CD-ROM published by the U.S. Department of Education.

The control/plurality cases that we used as a basis of comparison had slightly lower but statistically insignificant differences in mean turnout levels when compared to our experimental places. Before their adoption of CV, our experimental communities had averaged 18 percent turnout, which was comparable to 17 percent turnout for other plurality jurisdictions. Keeping with expectations about the effects of semi-PR rules on participation, turnout levels illustrated in these bivariate data were 5.5 percent higher in the experimental cases after their adoption of CV (23.5 percent). An ANOVA test determined that there were significant differences in turnout between these three categories ($F(2, 213) = 4.31$, $p = .015$). A t test used to calculate the magnitude of turnout difference between the mean turnout in places using CV/LV before and after election system change indicated that there was a significant difference between the two groups ($t = 2.64$, $p = .009$).[7] Since the turnout difference between the control and pre-experimental groups was not significant, these data suggest that it is unlikely that higher levels of turnout in the CV jurisdictions after election system changes resulted from factors at play prior to the adoption of CV.

Table 7.1 also demonstrates that despite our care in matching the demographics of the control group with the experimental group, some differences between the groups in terms of median income remained. Although the differences were not significant, they demonstrate the need to include demographic controls for median income in regression models of turnout. The data also illustrate that there was substantial variation in size of minority communities within each group. Since the size and type of minority community can affect turnout, it was necessary to determine whether our bivariate results would hold up when tested with regression models that included statistical controls for additional variables.

Hypotheses and Model Specification

The discussion above suggests several testable hypotheses. Clearly, if semi-PR election rules have any of the effects that scholars and advocates anticipate—mobilizing more candidates, making contests more competitive, or increasing voter efficacy—then turnout should be higher under CV when compared to elections held in similar places using plurality rules. Although we could not specify the actual mechanisms operating in CV elections that affect turnout, we could isolate the general effect of these election rules with a dummy variable, where 1 = a CV election (and in table 7.2 a CV or an LV election) and 0 = a plurality election. In cross-sectional models the coefficient for this represents the difference in turnout between plurality and CV places. In longitudinal models it represents the change in turnout after election rules switched to semi-PR.

Given the controls built into the case selection process and research design, we could be rather confident that this dummy variable captured differences between places that stemmed from different election rules. It was possible, however, that our case selection might not have fully controlled for variation in place-specific factors such as the racial composition of communities. Since we anticipated that communities with a larger proportion of Latino and/or African American residents might have lower turnout, independent of election system, our models included a variable that represented the proportion of voting-age residents who were nonwhite.

In addition to the relative size of the minority population in a community, the specific type of minority is also relevant. We anticipated that due to language barriers or citizenship status, Latinos simply did not turn out to vote at the same rate as African Americans or white voters. Indeed, several studies have found that Latinos turn out at relatively lower rates than whites and African Americans in various types of elections (Alvarez and Butterfield 2000; Stanley and Neimi 1995, 79; Uhlaner, Cain, and Kiewiet 1989). For this reason, we included a dummy variable that represented communities where Latinos were the largest minority group.[8] To control for further variation in the social composition of these places, we also included a measure of median income in the models. We assumed that places with higher median incomes would have more residents with the resources to participate in politics.[9]

We also included a dummy variable that distinguished between school board elections and elections to city and county councils. It is possible that voters take a more keen interest in council elections than school elections where these are held separately. Finally, there is reason to suspect that the size of a jurisdiction's population may have an impact on voter turnout. Larger places could feature different rates of voter participation for several reasons. Larger governments might provide more services to people, increasing what is at stake when offices are contested. These places could also feature more media outlets, bringing greater attention to local contests in populous places. Conversely, participation might be higher in smaller places due to easier organizing in small-scale places, or due to a "friends and neighbors" effect where there is greater personal familiarity with candidates in small places. Since there were relatively few cases in our analysis with populations over 100,000, there was an extreme rightward skew in the distribution of this variable. As a result, we found it necessary to use the log of population in the models estimated below.

Cross-Sectional Results

Table 7.2 reports the results of a set of OLS regression model of turnout. When all of our election turnout data were included in a single cross-sectional analysis—CV elections, plurality jurisdictions matched with these CV places (n = 216), and LV elections (n = 28)—we found that our model explained about half of the variation in local turnout. When controlling for the type of body being elected, the type of minority group dominant in the community, size of community, and size of the dominant minority population, we found that elections held under CV and LV were associated with about 4.5 percent higher turnout.

Table 7.3 displays estimations that utilize our quasi-experimental research design. We first estimated the model across all 216 elections in the data set to

TABLE 7.2. Cross-Sectional Models of Turnout in Local CV and LV Elections

	All CV and LV Elections
Minority % of population	−.159 * (.062)
Alternative elect. system	.045 ** (.014)
School board election	−.037 * (.014)
Latino community	−.241 ** (.024)
Population (logged)	−.026 ** (.008)
Median income	.000006 (.00002)
Intercept	.696 ** (.081)
R^2 (adjusted)	.482
Number of cases	244

Note: Dependent variable = turnout a proportion of voting age population.

** = $p < .01$, two-tailed.
* = $p < .05$, two-tailed.
+ = $p < .10$, two-tailed.

make a basic test of the effect of CV on turnout. The first model included 144 elections from all twenty-eight CV places from which we obtained data (seventy-four elections held before adopting CV, seventy after adopting CV), and seventy-two plurality elections from our twenty-one control places. This first model thus included elections from the seven CV places from which we obtained data without finding matching data from plurality jurisdictions. In the second model in table 7.3, we took advantage of our case selection design by estimating the model only with those 165 elections conducted in jurisdictions (twenty-one CV places and the twenty-one plurality places) where we had matched data on turnout and social and geographical traits. This set included sixty-three plurality elections from the control group, fifty plurality elections from places that would end up adopting CV, and fifty-two CV elections (see Appendix D).

Cross-sectional comparisons are further refined in the third and forth columns

TABLE 7.3. Cross-Sectional Models of Turnout in Local CV Elections

	All CV Elections	Matched by Place	Matched by Place & Time	Latino, Matched by Place and Time
Minority % of population	−.121 (.075)	−.098 (.093)	−.030 (.144)	.201 (.161)
Alternative elect. system	.051 ** (.015)	.050** (.019)	.047 + (.028)	.094 ** (.024)
School board election	−.028 + (.016)	−0.26 (.021)	−.007 (.034)	−.005 (.030)
Latino community	−.265 ** (.032)	−.223 ** (.039)	−.264 ** (.061)	—
Population (logged)	−.028 ** (.008)	−.029 ** (.010)	−.023 (.014)	−.004 (.021)
Median income	.00002 (.00002)	.00002 (.00003)	.00004 (.00003)	.00006 + (.00004)
Intercept	.685 ** (.080)	.605 ** (.097)	.526 ** (.141)	.111 (.235)
R^2 (adjusted)	.458	.318	.333	.090
Number of cases	216	164	82	64

Note: Dependent variable = turnout as a proportion of voting age population.

** = $p < .01$, two-tailed.
* = $p < .05$, two-tailed.
+ = $p < .10$, two-tailed.

of table 7.3. In the third column we limited the elections to those where turnout data for CV elections was matched with plurality elections in control jurisdictions, while also being matched such that forty-one CV elections were paired with forty-one plurality elections conducted in similar jurisdictions at the same time.[10] In the final column, the model was estimated with this same set but limited to those places where the predominant minority group was Latino. With this set of cases, we had thirty-two elections from CV places and thirty-two elections from matched plurality places.

For each model in table 7.3, the primary variable of interest is the dichotomous measure that indicates whether an election was run under alternative (semi-PR) rules. According to each of our cross-sectional estimates, elections held under CV did result in a significantly higher turnout rate than those run under traditional plurality schemes, with the effect of an alternative system ranging from 4.7 percent to 9.4 percent, depending on specification.[11] An increase of roughly 5 percent is a relatively modest impact due to system change (and our research design gives us some confidence in claiming that it is a system effect). In the context of local elections, this figure of 5 percent is even more impressive when the range of local turnout across these cases is considered.[12] For a jurisdiction having the mean turnout (19 percent), a 5 percent increase to 24 percent is, proportionately, a substantial increase in participation.

In the estimation including all elections, we found that there was an independent effect of the type of office being contested. When school board elections were held separately, fewer voters turned out. The log of population was also significant in the first two estimations. Although the log transformation rendered it difficult to discuss the substantive effects of the variable, the population variable was significant below the .01 level. We found that larger jurisdictions have lower turnout. This effect was reduced in estimations where the plurality and CV cases were most closely matched.[13] One possible explanation is that a large number of our elections were held in communities with populations no higher than several thousand. Elections may take on added meaning when your neighbor or a friend is running in the election, and small communities could have higher levels of "friends and neighbors" electioneering that acts to mobilize citizens. Finally, most models did not demonstrate any significant effect of median income on participation, although the direction of the coefficients suggests that wealthier communities have higher participation.

The models in table 7.3 also demonstrate that jurisdictions with Latinos as their primary minority group reported lower turnout rates when other factors were controlled for. The coefficient representing Latino communities is both substantively as well as statistically significant in each model. Indeed, the variable distinguishing between minority communities explains much of the variance in turnout—this is evident in the drop in model fit between the third and fourth estimations. When this variable is omitted from the analysis by limiting the estimation to Latino communities, the effect of election system remains significant while model fit drops to .09. A bivariate regression using the cases in column four produces a slope of .07 with nearly identical R^2. This suggests that while these semi-PR election systems are associated with explaining some variation in local turnout, the additive effect of population size, type of minority group, and type of electoral jurisdiction might explain even more variation across a large set of communities.

Longitudinal Results

The bivariate and cross-sectional results offer strong evidence that semi-PR local elections are associated with greater turnout than plurality elections in similar places. Our data also allowed us to test for the effects of electoral systems

TABLE 7.4. Longitudinal Models of Turnout in Local CV Elections

	All CV elections, Before and After	Elections Most Recent to Adoption of CV	Elections in Latino Communities, Most Recent to Adoption of CV
Minority % of population	–.123 (.077)	–.198+ (.116)	–.077 (.106)
Adoption of alt. elect. system	.040 ** (.016)	.054 * (.025)	.048 * (.022)
Latino	–.243 ** (.038)	–.218 ** (.056)	—
School board election	–.036 * (.018)	–.049+ (.029)	–.043 + (.024)
Population (logged)	–.050 ** (.011)	–.050 ** (.017)	–.044 ** (.017)
Median	–.00001 (.00003)	–.00009+ (.00006)	–.00006 (.00004)
Intercept	.880 ** (.091)	1.03 ** (.137)	.661 ** (.143)
R^2 (adjusted)	.461	.484	.288
Number of cases	144	65	56

Note: Dependent variable = turnout as a proportion of voting-age population. Recent elections include the three elections closest to adoption of CV (before and after).

** $p < .01$, two-tailed.
* $p < .05$, two-tailed.
+ $p < .10$, two-tailed.

over time by estimating our models using only elections from places that eventually adopted CV. Table 7.4 reports the results of three estimations of election system change on turnout. In these models the coefficient for alternative election system represents the intervention of the adoption of CV in each place and thus reflects the percentage increase in turnout after elections were conducted under semi-PR rules.

The first estimation made use of turnout data from 144 elections, seventy-four of which were held under plurality and the remaining seventy of which were conducted in the same jurisdictions after switching to CV. The second estimation used a similar set of cases but was limited to using no more than the three elections (plurality and CV) held most recent to the adoption of CV for each jurisdiction.[14] Finally, we estimated the longitudinal models with data from

Latino communities only, using data from elections held most recent to the switch in election systems.[15]

Most of the coefficients estimated in the longitudinal model (table 7.4) appear similar to the estimates from the cross-sectional analysis (tables 7.2 and 7.3). Of primary interest here is that the results for the effect of alternative election systems in table 7.4 are largely consistent with those reported in tables 7.2 and 7.3, ranging between a 4 and 5.4 percent increase after a jurisdiction ceases using plurality rules. Overall, the models in table 7.4 demonstrate that when we isolate a fixed set of jurisdictions in the United States and switch from plurality to semi-PR election rules we do see a significant increase in participation in elections. The effect is found within a set of places where many demographic and geographic factors are held constant by design.[16]

Although we cannot identify the micro-level foundations of this turnout increase, we embrace the theory discussed above and assume that CV elections either increase candidates' incentives to mobilize voters or increase voter efficacy (or both). There may, however, be another factor that explains why CV elections increase turnout. It is possible that there is some "novelty" factor associated with these elections that causes a short-term increase in participation. Voters could be attracted temporarily by the novelty of a system where they can vote three or five times for a single candidate but over time could grow bored of this new voting scheme and resume their preferred pattern of apathy. Likewise, mobilization efforts by local groups could be "one-shot" educational affairs that produce an increase in turnout only after the first semi-PR election.

Most jurisdictions used in this analysis adopted their alternative system as recently as 1994, and some only by 1998. This means that relatively few places have had a large series of successive CV elections. Yet it is still possible to use our data to test if turnout declined in CV places after the initial semi-PR election. First, we estimated our model of turnout using data from the sixty CV elections held in places that had more than one contest under semi-PR rules. We replaced the term for election system (since it would become a constant) with a variable representing the number of times a place had a CV election. Results (not reported) illustrated that the coefficient for election iteration was negative (-.005), but not at all significant ($p = .63$). In short, the increase in local election turnout demonstrated in our models does not appear to be the function of some short-lived novelty effect.

Discussion and Conclusion

Results presented in this chapter demonstrate that CV elections, and possibly LV elections, are associated with higher turnout than elections held under plurality rules. CV and LV thus offer the promise of increased representation of minorities coupled with increased participation in general. The size of the effect appears to be modest but noteworthy. A 4 to 5 percent boost in participation when relevant factors affecting participation are held constant by research design and by statistical controls is a meaningful one, especially when we consider the relatively low turnout rates in these kinds of elections. This effect may even be slightly larger in places where Latinos are the predominant minority, in part, we speculate, because there are more opportunities for turnout to increase in such places.

The multiple research designs that we have used with this data (quasi-experimental, controlled case selection, and correlational) all demonstrate that this is an institutional effect that cannot be dismissed as an artifact of an under-specified model that fails to control for place-specific (cultural, social, political, or geographic) factors. All of this suggests quite strongly that some underlying processes associated with CV and LV mobilize more voters than plurality elections. If political reformers are interested in increasing participation in U.S. elections, these findings could be taken as evidence that PR could stimulate greater participation, at least in local elections where the potential problem of low turnout is most severe.

Some advocates of electoral reform might find satisfaction in the link we found between institutional rules and participation. Yet these findings could also cast a shadow over claims advanced by some proponents of PR. If we can generalize from local elections in these mostly small jurisdictions, increased proportionality in electoral formula does not appear to be the magic bullet that will resolve problems of low participation in the United States. At the end of the day, rates of participation still seem low, and experimentation with other reforms, such as reintroducing partisan elections, may well be called for. While electoral institutions are only one of many small pieces of the puzzle of low turnout in the United States, at least these findings confirm that they are a piece of that puzzle.

Conceptually, the effect of these electoral institutions may be most apparent when we compare alternative systems with "majority-minority" SMD systems. Safe seats that result from drawing district boundaries may be expected to reduce both electoral competitiveness and voter turnout, but with one major gain, that districting advances the normative principle of descriptive representation of minorities. All electoral systems can be said to impose trade-offs, and the trade-off in districted approaches can be one where possible "losses" in participation are balanced against gains in descriptive representation. As we illustrated in this chapter, there are gains in participation under alternative electoral systems. It remains to be seen, however, whether gains in participation come along with gains in minority representation. That, of course, is the primary motive for experimenting with alternative election systems in the first place. If the strategic demands of CV and LV are too great for minority groups, or if mobilization of minority voters is inadequate, the gains in turnout that we identify here may be offset by potential losses in descriptive representation.

If the institutional choice is between minority representation with lower turnout (plurality SMD) and minority representation with slightly higher turnout (CV/LV), the findings of this chapter might be encouraging; but if the choice is between more turnout but less descriptively accurate representation, the choice becomes much harder. For those interested in securing minority representation where it has been lacking, a subtle increase in voter participation might not look very attractive if it does not correspond to actual seats for minority candidates. But if these alternative systems produce not only higher turnout but also increased descriptive representation, their appeal is consequently greater. The critical question, then, is, How do alternative electoral systems affect descriptive representation? We turn to this question in the next chapter.

· 8 ·

Minority Representation under Alternative Electoral Arrangements

Our overall goal has been to examine how election rules affect candidates, groups, their campaign activity, and voter mobilization. So far we have examined how electoral processes and activities in local campaigns are shaped by electoral systems, and we have demonstrated that local politics may differ between places using alternative versus standard plurality election rules. Our findings thus far establish that on some dimensions, cumulative voting (CV) elections are more competitive than plurality contests, that there are more efforts to mobilize voters under CV, and that voter turnout is higher under CV. When considered in relation to standard normative definitions of democratic practice, these findings suggest that CV may have much to offer.

We do, however, need to pay attention to the representation outcomes produced by election systems. The alternative systems we examine were implemented as explicit attempts to engage in electoral engineering with regard to outcomes. CV and LV were introduced with the express intent of increasing minority representation in ways that might avoid the problems and acrimony surrounding the use of majority-minority districts. We have provided a number of examples of communities electing racial and ethnic minorities for the first time under CV. It remains for us to establish the impact of these systems upon minority representation. Furthermore, since CV and LV are seen as alternatives to districting, we need to establish not just whether these alternative systems improve minority representation, but whether they do so in ways that are similar to or different from districting.

Our discussion of thresholds of exclusion illustrated that these alternative systems of CV and LV create opportunities for cohesive minority groups to win seats despite opposition from a majority of voters. With four seats contested under CV or LV, a cohesive minority candidate securing 20 percent of the vote cannot be excluded from winning a seat. Under at-large plurality rules, any candidate would require at least 50 percent to win a seat. Thus, compared to majoritarian plurality local elections, CV and LV create opportunities for greater representation of minorities. But there are also reasons to expect that CV or LV could possibly produce *less* proportional outcomes than those obtained under single-member simple-plurality (SMSP) districting, since minorities may have a difficult time overcoming those strategic obstacles. As we have seen, effective CV campaigns can require vote coordination efforts, limited nominations, and voter mobilization efforts, and voters must respond by turning out and plumping. Although we have shown that minority groups regularly respond to the strategic demands of CV, it is possible that SMSP majority-minority districting is more likely to automatically produce minority representation.

By contrast, under districting many of the problems of coordination and collective action are dealt with by the cartographers, who tailor boundaries so as to create heavily minority districts in proportion to the underlying population. Once these homogenous districts are created, almost no strategic behavior is required of elites or voters to ensure minority representation.[1] Whether alternative systems are well suited for producing minority representation at levels comparable to SMSP districting is an open matter, and outcomes depend, in part, upon the ability of minority voters and candidates to overcome the coordination problems posed by these alternative systems.

Expected Levels of Minority Representation under Various Election Systems

Our main empirical question here is whether minority candidates receive seats in local elections in rough proportion to a minority group's share of the local population. As we noted at the outset, the Voting Rights Act (VRA) was not designed with the explicit intent of achieving proportional representation (PR) of any minority group. Nevertheless, measures of the proportionality of the relationship between seats and population are standard for evaluating levels of minority representation in local elections (e.g., Engstrom and McDonald 1981). They also provide particular advantages by allowing us to compare observed rates of minority representation under CV and LV to other systems. Ideally, we would assess how election systems directly translate votes for minority candidates into seats, as this would give us the most accurate portrait of how systems might advantage or disadvantage certain voters. The privacy of the act of voting, however, means that data on votes cast by members of racial groups, and on the candidates they vote for, are simply unavailable over a large number of cases.[2] Tests using the seats-population relationship thus provide the best available method for comparing how various election systems translate support for minority candidates—albeit in this case potential support—into minority representation.

We advanced several testable propositions about how the seats-population relationship under alternative elections compares to those obtained under SMSP districting, and to unmodified at-large plans. We also assessed how LV and CV results compare to each other. First, we hypothesized that CV and LV should produce more proportionate representation of minorities than that resulting from the traditional plurality at-large elections that CV and LV replace. Assuming that a group votes roughly as a block, any group winning a plurality is likely to sweep all seats in an unmodified at-large election (Lakeman 1974). Although nearly every electoral system has bias in favor of the group gaining the largest vote share in an election, the bias is greatest under American-style at-large plurality systems (Johnson 1979). Conversely, both LV and CV have lower minimum thresholds than at-large elections, and Cox (1991) illustrated that outcomes under forms of LV in party systems can even be equivalent to d'Hondt PR under certain obtainable conditions.

Second, given strategic demands and the "semiproportionate" nature of CV/LV, we expected that these multimember district elections might produce less proportionate descriptive representation of minorities than SMSP districted elections. We did not expect that an electoral system using winner-take-all *without* race-based single-member districts would ever produce more proportionate outcomes than a multimember CV or LV system. It is important to note that the difference in proportionality we expected was not so much a function of SMSP districts per se as of the apportionment of racial and ethnic groups into particular districts. Alternative plans facilitate minority representation by lowering the threshold of votes required for a minority candidate to win office, but as we have shown, groups must be fairly well organized politically to take advantage of these systems. SMSP districted plans that take race into consideration when drawing district lines might facilitate minority representation with less coordination requirements for elites and voters.

Third, limited voting might be expected to produce a more proportionate seats-population relationship than cumulative voting. This hypothesis is based on the assumption that the latter system might require an additional element of strategic behavior (coordination of vote dispersion) from voters and elites.

Data and Analysis

As before, cases for our tests were drawn from U.S. cities, counties, and school districts that adopted CV or LV in response to actual or anticipated VRA lawsuits. Since we were interested in estimating how electoral systems were related to the representation of minority groups relative to their share of the local population, we limited our analysis to jurisdictions for which 1990 census population data were available. Initial information on local election systems and election results was obtained in the spring of 1995 via telephone interviews with city clerks and county election officials, with additional data acquired in subsequent interviews in 1996, 1997, and 1998. Nearly all the places we identified were located in three states: Texas, Alabama, and North Carolina. South Dakota, New Mexico, and Illinois also each had a single jurisdiction that used CV. We limited our analysis to places from these six states where the predominant minority made up less than 50 percent of the voting population. These were the same jurisdictions in which our candidate survey was conducted and the same places for which we sought data on turnout.[3]

We treated individual elections as cases. This allowed us greater comparability in our analysis, largely because this diffused the problem created by those jurisdictions that staggered elections. We included the two or three most recent elections from each jurisdiction in the analysis, or the most recent if the jurisdiction had only one CV or LV contest as of spring 1998. This allowed us to capture variation in elections across places and within places, since most of these communities alternated the number of seats contested in consecutive elections. Data from nearly all these places involved elections contested between 1994 and 1997, although the second most recent election in three places were held between 1990 and 1992.

The dependent variable was the percentage CV or LV seats won by minority candidates in each election. Our models thus isolated the seats-population relationship unique to CV and LV elections and eliminated from the analysis those seats elected in these communities by other methods.[4] Communities included in the seats-population analysis were limited to places with a population of over 1,000, the minimum for racial information to be included in census data. Most communities were rather small, with a median population of 3,152 and a mean of 10,235. The resulting sample used to assess the seats-population relationship included a total of sixty-five jurisdictions offering data for 118 elections.

Results: Evidence of Minority Electoral Success

Table 8.1 demonstrates that minority candidates have had success contesting these elections, despite their low levels of representation prior to the change in election systems. Consider the success of Latino candidates. We identified eighty-three contests that were conducted under alternative rules in places where the predominant minority was Latino. Latino candidates sought office in sixty of these places (72 percent of election contests in Latino CV places), and thirty-nine were elected. This meant that Latino candidates were elected in 65 percent of all CV contests where a Latino candidate sought office. Table 8.1 also illustrates

TABLE 8.1. Election of Minority Candidates under CV and LV

Predominant Minority Group	Total Number of Elections	Elections with Minority Candidates	Elections with Minority Victory
African American	32	30 (94%)	29(91%)[a] (97%)[b]
Latino	83	60 (72%)	39(47%)[a] (65%)[b]
Native American	03	02 (66%)	01(33%)[a] (50%)[b]
Totals	118	92 (78%)	69(58%)[a] (75%)[b]

Note: Cases are individual elections. Data are from elections as of 1997.

a. Percentage of all elections where minority candidate was elected.

b. Percentage of elections with minority candidates running where minority candidate was elected.

something that will be discussed below: In elections where the predominant minority was Latino, Latino candidates were not on the ballot in 28 percent of elections (see Appendixes E and F).

African American candidates were even more successful. We identified thirty-two separate CV and LV contests conducted in places where African Americans were the predominant minority group, and African American candidates sought office in thirty of these contests. In 97 percent of CV/LV elections where an African American sought office, at least one African American was elected. Case studies from jurisdictions electing Latino and African Americans under CV or LV illustrate that outside of Peoria, Illinois, there are no reasons to doubt that minority candidates elected were preferred by minority voters (see chapter 6).

It is important to stress that in nearly all of these places, no minority candidate had been able to win previously under plurality rules. For example, Thomas and Stewart (1988, 171) noted that 44 percent of Alabama Black Belt counties examined in a 1982 federal study (U.S. Civil Rights Commission, 1983) had no black representation—even counties that had majority-black populations. A number of our cases were drawn from these counties. Each of the North Carolina places using LV had also been in VRA-targeted areas since 1964. Keech and Sistrom (1994) reported that 90 percent of North Carolina counties and cities had traditional plurality at-large systems as of 1989, with blacks heavily underrepresented. In places where blacks were a minority, "representational equity scores" did not exceed .20, reflecting that minorities held very few seats relative to their share of the population. Nearly all of our North Carolina cases came from these communities. Brischetto (1995) also illustrated that CV elections in Texas resulted in victories for Latino and black candidates in places where these groups had rarely, if ever, won local office.

It is clear then, that minorities win seats under CV and LV, and that they win seats in places where plurality rules prevented prior representation. Little is known, however, about how systematic minority represenation is under CV and LV. Hypotheses about how elections translate minority voting-age population share into minority seats on local councils can be tested by regressing the percentage of seats on local councils held by minorities against the minority group's percentage share of the jurisdiction's population (Engstrom and McDonald 1981). Bivariate regression produces slope estimates that can be used to assess differences in seats-population relationships across electoral systems and can be compared to those produced by other studies using the same method. For example, when percentage data are used, a slope of 1.0 with an intercept of 0 indicates that minority seat shares on local councils occur in exact proportion to the percentage of the local voting-age population that is minority.

Due to the nature of our data, our analysis was slightly different than some studies of minority representation. Many studies now use regression models estimated with a universe of medium and large cities (i.e., all cities over 50,000). With such data, a single model can be specified with multiple intercepts and interaction terms to represent how different electoral systems affect the seats-population relationship. Interaction terms allow single-equation models to test if various electoral structures have different effects on minority council representation (Bullock 1994; Welch 1990, 1055; Engstrom and McDonald 1981, 347; Bullock and MacManus 1993).

Our data differed from these "larger N" studies in that our cases were election results from smaller places and our sample included responding communities from the universe of all known places above 1,000 population using CV or LV. Given the small number of cases, the unique characteristics of these communities, and the circumstances under which these election systems were adopted, we could not include multiple intercept terms that directly compared the seats-population relationship under LV and CV to that of other systems.

Models were first estimated for all CV and LV jurisdictions, including all 118 CV and LV elections where the predominate minority group could either be African American, Latino, or Native American[5] (model 1). We then estimated separate models for African American and Latino places to assess if CV and LV were associated with a different seats-population relationship for these groups (models 2 and 3, respectively). We also estimated a multivariate model with all cases using an interaction term and dummy variable to test if minority representation was more common under LV than CV (model 4). To evaluate our other hypotheses, the slopes resulting from these models were compared to those produced from other studies. This could provide some idea of how minority representation under modified at-large elections compared to other electoral systems used in U.S. localities.

Information about the slope of these relationships can be more important than a simple demonstration that more minorities serve on these local councils after changing to CV or LV. Each of these jurisdictions adopted new electoral systems because they had sizable minority populations with very limited (or in many places no) minority representation. Only two of these places had minority populations under 10 percent (the lowest being 7 percent). Our models illustrate the systematic relationship between a minority group's potential electoral strength and its success in securing seats in a manner that facilitates comparison with studies of other electoral systems.

Minority Seats-Population Relationships: Results

Results from model 1 indicate that when elections from *all* CV and LV jurisdictions were examined simultaneously, there was no fit between minority population and percentage of seats controlled by the minority groups. Systematic variation in seats-population relationships across alternative election jurisdictions, however, was evident when we examined African American and Latino jurisdictions separately. The fit of the model was greatly improved (R^2 = .27) when elections contested in African American jurisdictions were examined in isolation (the R^2 increased to .45 when the analysis was restricted to cases with black candidates) (see table 8.2). Model 2 illustrates that for these places, the relationship between seats and minority voting-age population was represented by a slope of .95 and an intercept not significantly different from 0. Recall that a slope of 1.0 represents a perfectly proportionate relationship between potential minority electoral strength and levels of minority representation. Thus, in those CV/LV elections where the primary minority was African American, as the minority percentage of the population increased, a nearly equivalent gain in descriptive representation was achieved. Furthermore, since the intercept was near 0, population share was translated into representation at low levels of minority population.

The systematic relationship between minority population share and minority seat size was less apparent in jurisdictions where Latinos were the predominant minority. Model 3 reports the slope of the seats-population relationship for places where the predominate minority was Latino. Given the insignificant slope and the very low R^2, there does not appear to be a substantive linear relationship between

TABLE 8.2. Minority Seats—Population Relationship under CV and LV

	Model 1	**Model 2**	**Model 3**	**Model 4**
	(All)	(Black)	(Latino)	(LV)
Variables:				
Minority %VAP	.17	.95***	.09	.06
	(.13)	(.26)	(.21)	(.16)
LV Dummy	—	—	—	–.17
				(.16)
LV * Min%VAP	—	—	—	1.05**
				(.51)
Intercept	.15**	.04	.14	.15**
	(.06)	(.06)	(.07)	(.05)
R^2	.01	.27	.00	.09[a]
N	118	32	83	118

Note: Dependent variable = proportion of CV/LV council seats won by minority candidates.

[a]R^2 for model 4 is adjusted; all others unadjusted.

***$p < .01$ **$p < .05$ (all two-tailed t-tests)

minority population share and minority seat share on councils and school boards. This does not mean that Latino candidates were not elected in places that adopted modified at-large voting. As with African American jurisdictions, Latino candidates were elected in greater numbers after switching to a modified at-large system. As reported in table 8.1, where Latino candidates sought office, they were successful in over half (39 out of 60) of these cases, marking a dramatic improvement over previous levels of Latino representation in these communities (Brischetto 1995; Brischetto and Engstrom 1997). Nevertheless, elections in many places with substantial Latino populations produced no Latino representation due to a lack of candidates or defeat at the polls. Even when the analysis was restricted to cases where Latino candidates sought office (not reported here), there was still no significant effect. This does not mean that there was no systematic relationship between Latino *vote* share and Latino representation under CV. In the next section we address how standard seats-*population* models can easily underestimate the potential for Latino representation.

We hypothesized that these new CV/LV systems would produce more proportionate descriptive representation of minorities than plurality at-large plans and less proportionate representation than SMSP districted plans. Our results are put into perspective by comparing the parameters from our models to those from other studies examining U.S. local election systems. If we compare our slope and intercept for African American representation under CV/LV systems to

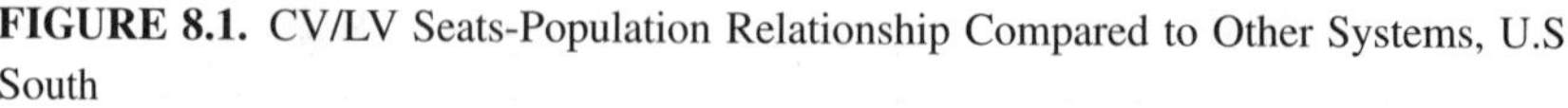

FIGURE 8.1. CV/LV Seats-Population Relationship Compared to Other Systems, U.S. South

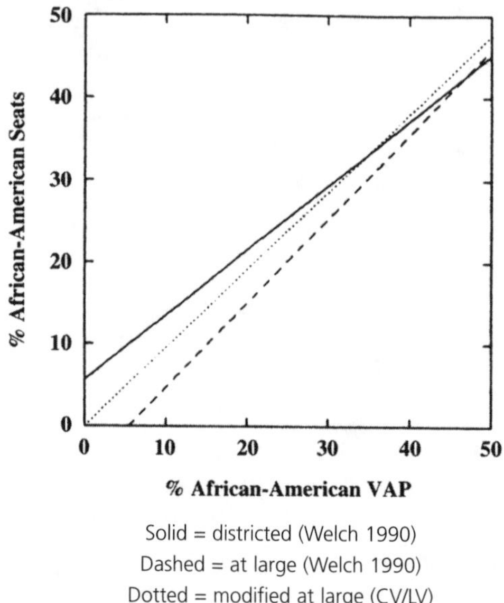

Solid = districted (Welch 1990)
Dashed = at large (Welch 1990)
Dotted = modified at large (CV/LV)

slopes estimated from previous studies of plurality at-large systems, we find some support for these hypotheses.

As figure 8.1 illustrates, the seats-population relationship for African Americans under recently CV or LV systems is similar to that found by Welch (1990) for African Americans in larger (over 50, 000 residents) southern cities using SMD where blacks are a minority of the population. Figure 8.1 compares our results from model 2 to Welch's findings. Across much of the range in minority population, it appears that modified (CV/LV) plans (represented by the dotted line) produce similar levels of representation to districting (the solid line), and slightly greater descriptive representation than plurality at-large plans (the dashed line).

Since nearly all of our cases came from elections in relatively small places that recently switched election systems, Welch's data might not be best suited for comparing seat-population relationships across systems. When we compared our estimates to those from a study of other southern places that had recently switched away from at-large plans, where the analysis included many smaller, rural places more similar to communities in our study, levels of African American representation under CV/LV appeared more striking. Bullock (1994) examined elections to county commissions in Georgia in 1991. Fifty-two of these counties used SMSP district plans, an increase from 17 in 1981.[6] Figure 8.2 plots Bullock's bivariate seats-registration relationship in SMD places (the solid

FIGURE 8.2. CV/LV Seats-Population Relationship Compared to Other Systems, U.S. South

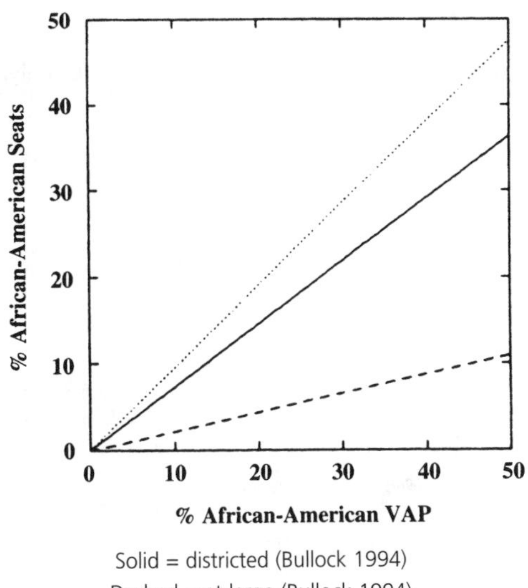

Solid = districted (Bullock 1994)
Dashed = at large (Bullock 1994)
Dotted = modified at large (CV/LV)

line), and the relationship we estimated in model 2 for African American jurisdictions using CV/LV plans (the dotted line). The plot demonstrates results contrary to one of our hypotheses: modified at-large elections actually produced slightly *more* proportionate outcomes when compared to these districted places.

The differences between plurality at-large elections and CV/LV elections were substantial when we compared our estimates to those from Bullock's study of Georgia counties and were consistent with the hypothesis that CV/LV plans would produce more proportionate representation of minorities than plurality at-large systems. The dashed line represents the bivariate seats-registration relationship for the forty-one Georgia counties still using unmodified at-large elections in 1991. Compared to these cases, CV/LV produced substantially greater descriptive representation for African Americans.[7]

Our last hypothesis dealt with the difference between outcomes under LV versus CV systems. Since LV plans might involve fewer strategic burdens (vote dispersion coordination), we expected that LV systems could produce greater minority representation than CV. Model 4 included a coefficient reflecting the interaction between a dummy representing LV places and minority voting-age population. In theory, this coefficient isolates the unique seats-population relationship for LV. The significant coefficient for the interaction term (1.05, $p < .05$) can be seen as reflecting greater proportionate descriptive representation

TABLE 8.3. African American Seats-Population Relationship under CV and LV

Variables	Model 5 (CV only)	Model 6 (LV only)
Minority % voting-age population	.65 ** (.20)	1.12 * (.61)
Intercept	.08 ** (.02)	−.02 (.19)
R^2	.43	.19
N	15	17

Note: Dependent variable = proportion of CV/LV council seats won by minority candidates.

* $p < .10$, two-tailed. ** $p < .05$, two-tailed.

of minorities when comparing LV to CV places. This is consistent with assumptions that lower strategic demands are required for effective use of LV.

It is important to stress that there were relatively few cases of LV elections here ($n = 17$) and that all were in places where the predominant minority was African American.[8] The interaction in model 4 could possibly capture the difference between African American representation under LV and Latino and African American representation under CV.

Another way to determine if minorities achieve higher representation under LV is to estimate the seats-population slope for African Americans unique to places using CV (model 5) and then compare this to the slope for African American places using LV (model 6). These results are reported in table 8.3. We found weak evidence suggesting a more proportionate (or overproportionate) relationship between minority population and seats in LV elections ($b = 1.12$, $p = .08$) than in CV elections ($b = .65$, $p < .05$).[9] However, the population-seats coefficient under LV was not significantly larger than coefficient under CV. The slope and intercept values for the population-seats model in table 8.3 does suggest that CV communities elected black candidates at about the same rate as the districted places analyzed by Bullock as black populations approached 50 percent. At lower ranges of black population, the intercept from model 5 indicates that places with CV produced greater representation than Bullock's SMD places.

There are many additional elements of election system variation that cannot be captured by these dummy variables (degree to which vote is limited, proportion of all seats elected CV or LV, years that jurisdiction has been using CV or LV, etc.). Given limited degrees of freedom here, we cannot include these terms and thus cannot conclude with certainty that LV as practiced in the United States produces more proportionate representation of minorities than CV. Under either plan, however, minority seat share increases as minority population increases.

We should note that there are reasons to expect that the number of seats being contested should affect proportionality for any election system (Lijphart 1994). We did include this as an independent variable in preliminary models, but the effect was not significant. Since our goal was replicating models from other studies that did not include this measure, we do not include the term in models reported here. There was limited variance in number of seats contested among these elections, so it was difficult to evaluate the effect of this variable.

Latino Representation under Cumulative Voting

Our results from Latino places raise questions about why CV election outcomes were less than proportionate in these estimations of the seats-population relationship. In the cases examined here, underproportionality reflected by our estimates could be a function of three main factors. First, as seen in table 8.1, there was limited recruitment of Latino candidates. In almost one-third of CV jurisdictions where Latinos were the predominant minority, no Latino candidates sought office. More Latinos seek office in places after the switch to CV, and more are elected (Brischetto and Engstrom 1997), but Latinos do not win seats in proportion to their share of population. Second, and related to this, there is a substantial gap between census measures of Latino voting-age *population* (the key independent variable in these models) and actual rates of *participation* by Latino citizens in elections. Third, there is a relatively high threshold of exclusion built into many of the CV plans adopted by places where Latinos are the predominant minority. We examine each of these explanations below.

Among our cases were a number Texas CV elections (n = 44) having substantial Latino populations but achieving no Latino representation. In 23 of these cases, local officials indicated that no minority candidates had filed for office. Likewise, there were only two cases where African Americans constituted the predominant minority group and no African American candidate sought office. Since the data reveal that the nomination problem was more substantial for Latino jurisdictions, undernomination can partially explain the lack of a linear relationship between seats and population share in Latino jurisdictions.

But even when we account for undernomination, Latino candidates are still not elected at rates matching their share of the population. We can see this by selecting out only those sixty elections where Latino candidates sought office (model 7 in table 8.4). The slope of the seats-population line is 0, and the intercept is well above 0. This is because there were twenty-one cases where Latino candidates were defeated in places with significant Latino populations.

TABLE 8.4. Latino Representation under Cumulative Voting, Estimated by Population, Registration, and Relative Participation: Places with Latino Candidates

Variables	Model 7 (population)	Model 8 (registration)	Model 9 (relative to threshold)	Model 10 (as share of electorate)
Latino % voting-age population	.01 (.24)	—	—	—
Latino % Reg.	—	.01 (.009)	—	—
Latino % relative to threshold of exc.	—	—	.50** (.08)	—
Latino % of all voters	—	—	—	2.03** (.45)
Intercept	.24** (.08)	−.03 (.24)	−.14* (.07)	−.14 (.10)
R^2	.00	.11	.78	.63
N	60	14	14	14

Note: Dependent variable = proportion of CV seats won by Latino candidates.

Source: Model 7, authors' data. Models 8–10, Brischetto and Engstrom (1997, 983,985).

* = significant at $p < .05$

** = significant at $p < .01$

This suggests that overnomination, although a problem, was not the primary reason for low levels of estimated Latino representation in our seats-population models.

A second major factor affecting our ability to estimate representation of Latinos under CV is the use of census measures of voting-age population. In most of the places included in this analysis, Latino turnout was far lower than white turnout and lower than census measures of Latino voting-age population. In two of these jurisdictions, however, minority turnout actually exceeded Anglo turnout and minority candidates were elected (Brischetto and Engstrom 1997). Percent minority voting-age population data are likely to produce a lower estimated slope than would result if registration or turnout data were used, since these latter variables more accurately reflect minority electoral strength. Brischetto and Engstrom (1997) assumed the laborious task of assembling lists of Latino surname registration and Latino voter participation from the voter rolls from fourteen local CV elections contested in Texas in 1995. These data allowed a rare opportunity to assess how actual levels of minority voter mobilization affect minority representation across jurisdictions.[10]

Model 8 in table 8.4 estimates the proportion of seats won in these 1995 Texas elections with Latino registration and Latino turnout. The results illustrate that higher rates of Latino registration do not produce systematic gains in Latino representation in isolation from higher rates of Latino participation. The effect of Latino participation on seats won by Latino candidates is reflected in models 9 and 10. Model 9 estimates the proportion of seats won by Latinos as a function of Latino turnout relative to a jurisdiction's threshold of exclusion. The positive, significant slope for this term illustrates that more Latino candidates were elected when Latino turnout rates approached or exceeded the jurisdiction's threshold. When Latino turnout as a share of the participating electorate was used to estimate Latino seat share (model 10), the slope for the Latino seats-participation relationship was 2.03 (R^2 = .63), and the result was statistically significant. Thus, for every 1 percent increase in Latino participation as a proportion of the electorate, Latinos won 2 percent more in seat share. This demonstrates the critical importance of voter mobilization efforts under CV: Latino candidates do particularly well under CV when Latino voters are mobilized, but they win relatively few seats when participation levels are low. Nevertheless, there is a systematic relationship between Latino participation and Latino representation that is masked when census measures of population are used to estimate Latino seat share.

Compounding this is a third factor. Most places in Texas tended to have only two or three CV seats up in any single election. All but two of the Latino cases in our data set came from Texas. This means that the threshold of exclusion was typically either 25 percent or 33 percent in Texas. Low levels of minority participation will be particularly problematic when the threshold is this high.

Discussion

Our findings in this chapter provide evidence that CV and LV elections offer the promise of minority representation at levels very similar to those found under SMSP districting plans, including those where districting plans take race into consideration. This finding should be encouraging to those interested in facilitating minority representation without relying upon the acrimonious and litigious process of drawing districts on the basis of race. Previous research and discussions in earlier chapters have established that minorities do win seats under these alternative plans. Our purpose here was to identify how the seats-population relationship under CV-LV compared to those produced under other plans. For African Americans, representation from CV-LV elections compared favorably to that obtained from SMSP districts in similar places and was more proportionate relative to population than representation under plurality at large. For Latinos in communities studied here, this might not be the case. However,

Latinos were quite successful in winning seats, and they won more seats systematically, when Latino voters were mobilized.

We should stress that factors explaining lower rates of Latino representation relative to population are not an automatic result of the use of CV electoral systems. Given issues of citizenship and registration, models using population measures will underestimate the systematic nature of Latino success under CV. Furthermore, there are constraints in how some CV and LV plans were designed. If no more than two seats are contests in an election, it will be difficult for any minority to gain seats unless the minority votes as a block, controls a relatively large share of voting-age population (near or greater than 33 percent), *and* mobilizes voters to turn out at rates matching or exceeding the majority group's voters.

If, however, the election plan creates a threshold that does not exceed the minority group's electoral strength, and a minority political group is organized such that it can recruit candidates, perhaps have some control over nominations, and/or mobilize voters to direct all their votes to specific candidate(s), then many of the strategic burdens associated with CV/LV can be overcome. Our results suggest that these burdens are clearly surmountable and that CV/LV plans do facilitate proportionate descriptive representation of minority groups under easily obtainable conditions.

·9·

Conclusions about the Consequences of Minority Representation via Cumulative Voting

Our study demonstrates that cumulative voting (CV) has a great deal to offer as a method of facilitating minority representation. In fact, our empirical findings lead us to believe that it may do a better job of producing minority representation than majoritarian elections, including those that use race-conscious districting. CV elections mobilize candidates; this, in turn, makes campaigns more active, and that, in its turn, mobilizes voters. Where minority representation is produced via race-based districting, groups and candidates need not be as active to achieve descriptive representation. Even if outcomes are the same under both CV and districted approaches, the process of elections and electioneering is still quite different. But CV also seems to produce more accurate descriptive representation than districting, in part as a consequence of these different behaviors by candidates.

The fact that we find these effects in relatively small jurisdictions should not make them seem unimportant. As we have argued, the strategic demands associated with contesting a CV election require that groups and candidates be active and organized in order to win. These demands will exist at any level that this election system is used, whether for a special local district, a town council, or for the U.S. Congress. If anything, we would expect that minority groups would be even better positioned to take advantage of CV if it were used to elect a state's legislature or a state's congressional delegation. At these higher levels of politics it is likely that preexisting political groups would be in a position to coordinate elite and mass behavior and mobilize supporters, while CV's capacity for crossover voting makes the Balkanization of politics less likely.

Up to this point we have simply assumed that descriptive representation of minority groups is a good thing regardless of the method used to achieve it. This assumption, shared by many, is derived from our normative sense of fairness.

And if we are simply interested in producing representation for one or two minority groups that are physically segregated from whites and from each other, race-conscious districting is an easier and more certain option. We assume that citizens should be able to elect descriptive representatives if they want to.[1] But there are other reasons to be interested in descriptive representation; representation itself may affect how minority citizens view their political world and whether they continue to participate in politics.

Below, we examine if descriptive representation of minorities has effects that shape the political attitudes and behavior of the individuals who gain representation. We test if African Americans who have African American representatives in Congress are more likely to see government as responsive and are more likely to vote than African Americans who have white representatives. Results showing this would suggest that descriptive representation has effects that extend even beyond our conceptions of democratic fairness. Following this, we conclude with a discussion of why CV—or any "ordinal" election plan—might be a better way to produce minority representation in the U.S. Congress and other legislative bodies.

Minority Representation and Political Empowerment: A Spillover Effect

What positive spillover effect does representation by a minority legislator have on the attitudes and behavior of minority voters? Although we cannot answer this directly from the communities under study here, we can make use of survey data from the American National Election Study (ANES) to examine this in the context of representation in the U.S. House of Representatives.

Bobo and Gilliam (1990; see also Tate 1994) suggested that minority citizens could become "empowered" after they achieve visible influence in political decision making. They reasoned that such empowerment should influence participation because the presence of minority representatives creates cues that affect how citizens perceive the value of voting (379). These cues signal likely policy responsiveness "that encourages minorities to feel that participation has intrinsic value" (387). Using a rare survey that oversampled African Americans, they found that African American citizens in or near cities with an African American mayor were more efficacious and more likely to participate. We do not know, however, how far we might generalize beyond this finding[2] or whether the effects of empowerment extend to legislative settings.

Descriptive representation in a legislature may affect the attitudes and behavior of African Americans, due to what Mansbridge (1999, 642) identified as the "communicative advantages" of such representation. Without a descriptive representative, many nonwhite constituents face barriers communicating and identifying with their representative. In contrast, the presence of a descriptive representative can break down such barriers. Mansbridge cited as an example Richard Fenno's portrait (1978) of an African American congressman's interactions with his constituents: "every expression he gives or gives off conveys the idea 'I am one of you'" (115; see also Swain 1993, 219). This style of representation might cause African American constituents with African American representatives to be more likely to contact their legislator than African American constituents represented by white legislators (Gay 1997).

Tests of the effect of minority empowerment in legislative settings have been constrained by data availability. We addressed this by pooling opinion data from several congressional elections into a single data set (including 1990, 1992, 1994, 1996, and 1998 from the ANES).[3] This allowed us to identify a reasonable number of African Americans who are represented by an African American.[4] In doing this, we could compare African Americans represented by African Americans to other African Americans and to whites.[5] Our resulting samples included 1,052 African Americans. Twenty-eight percent were empowered in the sense that they were represented by an African American at the time they were surveyed.

We used responses to standard questions about political efficacy and participation to model the effects of minority empowerment via legislative representation. The statement "People like me don't have any say about what government does" was used as a measure of the perceived responsiveness of government. Higher values indicated more positive attitudes toward government. Participation was measured by responses to a question asking if the respondent voted.

In tables 9.1 and 9.2 we model the effects of African American empowerment on attitudes about government responsiveness and voting, respectively. The main effect of minority empowerment is coded with a dummy variable reflecting African Americans having an African American representative. This main dummy variable allowed us to assess the difference between African Americans with a descriptive representative and African Americans with a white representative.

Our models also control for the effects of factors expected to influence attitudes about government, including level of education, the absence of party attachments, gender, age, income, evaluations of the economy, propensity to attend religious services, and place of residence. We also include a dummy variable for southerners. We include dummy variables for election year to control for election-specific effects, with 1992 being the reference category. We assume that individuals who were represented by someone of the same party would have more positive views about politics and governmental responsiveness, so we include a variable to control for this effect (Identify w/ Party of Rep.). The models also include a term for the interaction between education and empowerment to test if descriptive representation had a greater impact among the least educated voters.

TABLE 9.1. Effect of Minority Representation on Attitudes about Government Responsiveness, OLS Estimates

	Coef.	s.e.
African Amer. rep.	0.81 **	0.29
African Amer. rep. * Educ.	–0.19 **	0.08
Contacted by party	0.25 *	0.12
Education	0.21 **	0.04
Ident. w/party as rep.	0.00	0.13
Independent	0.10	0.18
Female	–0.15	0.10
Age (in 10s)	0.02	0.03
Income	0.02 *	0.01
Economy	0.03	0.05
Attend religious svc.	–.0.22 *	0.11
Urban residence	0.12	0.10
South	0.05	0.10
1990	–0.60 **	0.15
1994	–0.72 **	0.16
1996	–0.28	0.17
1998	–0.39	0.20
Constant	2.21 **	0.26
Adjusted R^2	0.12	
Number of cases	866	

Note: Dependent variable is 1 if respondent voted, 0 if otherwise. Cell entries are logistic regression coefficients.

Source: American National Election Studies (1990, 1992, 1994, 1996, 1998).

* $p < .05$, two-tailed.

** $p < .01$, two-tailed.

Results of our estimation of attitudes about responsiveness were consistent with the empowerment thesis. Table 9.1 demonstrates that for African American respondents, the main effect of having an African American representative (.81) was significant. Thus, when these other factors were held constant, African Americans with African American representatives found government to be more responsive than African Americans with white representatives. The negative sign for the interaction coefficient (-.19) illustrates that the effect of descriptive representation on African American respondents' feelings of responsiveness declined as education increases. This interaction effect suggests that descriptive representation was associated with more positive perceptions of government responsiveness among African Americans with the lowest levels of education.

Table 9.2 reports the results of a logistic regression model estimating the effect of empowerment on the likelihood of voting. An additional variable (Con-

TABLE 9.2. Effect of Minority Representation on Voting: Logistic Regression Estimates of Reported Participation in Elections

	Coef.	s.e.
African Amer. rep.	1.43 **	0.52
African Amer. rep. * Educ.	–0.43 **	0.14
Contacted by party	1.21 **	0.24
Education	0.58 **	0.08
Ident. w/party as rep.	0.52 *	0.23
Independent	–0.33	0.32
Female	0.14	0.17
Age (in 10s)	0.47 **	0.06
Income	0.03*	0.01
Economy	–0.10	0.08
Attend religious svc.	0.64 **	0.19
Urban residence	0.22	0.18
South	–0.28	0.18
1990	–1.72 **	0.27
1994	–1.25 **	0.27
1996	–0.32	0.30
1998	–1.05 **	0.35
Constant	3.76 **	0.49
Nagelkerke R^2	0.37	
Number of cases	871	
Cases correctly classified	72.3	
–2 log likelihood	908.7	

Note: Dependent variable is 1 if respondent voted, 0 if otherwise. Cell entries are logistic regression coefficients.

Source: American National Election Studies (1990, 1992, 1994, 1996, 1998).

* $p < .05$, two-tailed.

** $p < .01$, two-tailed.

tacted by Party) was included to control for the effects of voter mobilization efforts. We found that an African American with a descriptive representative had a significantly higher likelihood of having voted than an African American with a white representative. This complements our finding that CV elections have mobilizing effects, for it suggests that after minorities secure representation (via any election plan), descriptive representation may lead them to participate at higher rates than minority citizens who lack descriptive representation.[6] This has broader implications, since these empowered minority voters will influence other contests on the ballot when they vote. Again, the interaction term suggests that this effect might be greatest at lower levels of education.

It is important to note that we conducted other tests that found that descriptive representation did not correspond with less cynicism about government.[7]

Nevertheless, our basic results are consistent with the empowerment thesis: we found that descriptive representation led minority citizens to see government as being more responsive "to people like me" and led them to vote more than other minority citizens.

Of course, these tests reflect the effect of descriptive representation via single-member districted (SMD) congressional districts. We propose that this is a general effect of descriptive representation. It can be caused by a mayoral election, a gubernatorial election, or a legislative election and thus is not unique to SMD legislative elections. We expected that empowerment effects in legislative settings would be heightened if minority representatives were elected via CV, since, as we have demonstrated, CV elections would require even more interaction between a representative's campaign and the voter. This could cause citizens to perceive that public officials were more responsive to their concerns. Furthermore, by requiring greater mobilization efforts, CV elections could have an even greater impact on minority citizens' propensity to vote.

Minority Influence as a Spillover Effect of Cumulative Voting

Lani Guinier and other advocates of CV argue that the beneficial effects of descriptive representation via CV elections—and other ordinal voting systems such as single transferable vote (STV)—can extend even further. We have stressed the competitive electoral advantages of CV in particular and the positive attitudinal and behavior effects of descriptive minority representation generally. Guinier noted that legislatures (or local councils) elected by CV may also provide a minority representative with more influence than he or she would achieve in a legislature elected by majoritarian rules.

In a CV body, white and nonwhite representatives alike stand a good chance of being elected with votes from both white and nonwhite voters. This is the one characteristic of any ordinal voting system: voters can spread their support across multiple candidates. Whites can vote for whites *and* nonwhites if they choose not to plump. Nonwhites can vote for nonwhites *and* whites if they choose not to plump. This means that once elected via CV, white and nonwhite representatives may be more likely to have some common ground, at least in terms of the constituents who put them in office. In contrast, representatives elected from racially homogeneous districts are almost predetermined to have no such common ground. This becomes more problematic as the districts of majority representative become more homogeneously white, since the white representative will have little electoral incentive to consider the interests of a minority representative. This is the zero-sum nature of districting.

The issue of minority influence in legislative bodies elected under "consensual" versus majoritarian rules presents the next major research question for those who are interested in examining how electoral reform might promote minority rights in the United States. Unfortunately, we do not have data that allow us to test whether a minority representative has more substantive influence if elected via CV or via SMD. However, examples from CV elections discussed in previous chapters do demonstrate that white candidates are regularly elected with some nonwhite support in CV contests and that nonwhite candidates regularly receive some white support. Exit polls from Alamogordo, New Mexico, for example, found that 27 percent of Latino voters supported white candidates and that 22 percent of whites supported the Latina candidate (Cole, Taebel, and Engstrom 1990, 195–97). Examples from Peoria, Sisseton, and Amarillo also illustrate that minority voters are more likely than whites to plump but that many minority voters spread their support across a number of white and nonwhite candidates.[8]

Thus, empirical observations suggest that voters do behave in ways that may cause CV to produce legislative bodies with minority representatives and with white representatives who depend on minority voters for some of their support. If they are sensitive to the voters who supported them, these white representatives elected by CV may be more sensitive to nonwhite interests expressed by a minority representative. A similar effect may operate with "minority influence" U.S. House districts, where a minority group allies with whites to elect a white representative. Ordinal voting plans such as CV, however, can produce both descriptive representation and (subtle) minority influence over white representatives even on relatively small councils and in settings where minority populations are dispersed. Given demographic trends in the U.S. discussed in the first chapter, this latter point in particular is another reason for considering CV as a means for electing state congressional delegations.

Prospects for the Use of CV in the Future

Until *Shaw v. Reno* (1993) and associated court decisions that challenged the use of race as an overriding criterion in drawing districts for the U.S. House, SMD was the only serious electoral system option considered for advancing minority representation in Congress and in U.S. states and communities. It is clear that districts are effective at promoting equitable outcomes (for some) in terms of descriptive representation. Since *Shaw,* however, critiques of the use of districting have accelerated.

Yet representative bodies elected via SMDs—and majoritarian elections generally—can produce minority representation at a relatively high cost. Majoritarian systems may generate different processes of mass participation than other systems (Powell 1986; Blais and Carty 1990); may encourage some voters to defect from their most preferred candidate (Riker 1982); may encourage personal rather than issue- or party-based campaigning (Bowler, Farrell, and McAllister 1996); and can exclude minorities from much legislative action once they are represented (Guinier 1994). At a more practical level, it also becomes difficult and costly to draw homogeneous districts that minorities can win in places where residents are not segregated by race or ethnicity.

We have addressed a problematic question faced by many democracies: How should election rules be engineered to best incorporate and accommodate minorities into legislatures? At present, nearly all U.S. legislatures are elected via majoritarian/plurality arrangements, with most minority representation occurring as a result of spatial concentrations of populations in districts. In the post-*Shaw* environment, however, scholars, journalists, members of the legal community, politicians, interest groups such as the American Civil Liberties Union, civil rights groups, and minority voting rights activists have began to look seriously at CV and limited voting (LV) as alternatives to districting.[9]

At the time of this writing, it seems that momentum is growing for use of alternative elections. In at least three instances, a U.S. District Court ordered CV as a remedy in vote dilution suits.[10] In September 1999, the House Judiciary Subcommittee on the Constitution held a hearing on the States' Choice of Voting Systems Act (HR 1173), a bill that would allow the election of state congressional delegations by multimember districts via CV, LV, or STV—in essence, allowing states to conduct experiments similar to those examined in this study. Robert Ritchie, director of the Center for Voting and Democracy, a Washington, D.C.–based group that advocates electoral reform, believes that STV and "instant runoff" voting might even be more politically acceptable for the United States than CV.[11] STV has a history of use in U.S. cities, is currently in use in Cambridge, Massachusetts, and is used to elect thirty-two community school boards in New York City. Moreover, referendum proposals to adopt STV in Cincinnati (in 1988 and 1991) and San Francisco (in 1996) received about 45 percent support on average (see Ritchie and Hill 1999).

A state could use CV, or STV, to elect all or part of its congressional delegation. We could see multimember congressional districts elected by CV or STV as being particularly attractive in socially diverse urban settings. One critique of the use of these alternative election plans to elect U.S. House delegations is that constituents desire a representative drawn from their particular geographic area. If districts were elected statewide, a representative's links to a locality might be weakened. The use of multimember districts to elect part of a state's delegation in regions such as Los Angeles, Miami, or Houston, however, would not be too far removed from standard conceptions of geographic representation.

Although the States' Choice of Voting Systems Act was not passed, an official from the Clinton administration testified in support, stating, "The Department of Justice supports this legislation as a valuable way to give state legislatures additional flexibility in the redistricting process" (Center for Voting and Democracy [CVD] 2000). As noted, in May 2000, Amarillo, Texas, held a school board election and became the largest U.S. jurisdiction to use CV. Amarillo adopted CV as part of the settlement of a vote dilution suit filed by the National Association for the Advancement of Colored People and the League of United Latin American Citizens. Whatever the nature of this momentum, CV and LV remain little-used election systems.

As we have demonstrated, these alternative systems do have much to offer. But the relative merits of CV/LV extend beyond simple calculations of rates of minority representation. We must stress that there are practical matters that will probably trump any short-term move away from single-member simple-plurality (SMSP) systems in the United States, particularly in congressional elections. There is simply no sense of national urgency or crisis that might accelerate reform at present.

At least two trends might affect moves toward electoral system reform in the United States in the future, however. First, if forthcoming reapportionments and redistricting (2002, 2012) are increasingly "race neutral" and if some measure of racially polarized voting continues, we can expect the proportion of minorities in Congress to decline. In the long run, this could lead to new pressure for change from groups losing descriptive representation.

Second, categories of race and minority status, and identity based on these concepts, might become more complex in the twenty-first century as newer groups increase their proportion of the population and more citizens identify themselves as multiracial or mixed race. The race question on new census forms includes the instruction "Mark one or more races." In effect, this allows the expression of complex preferences in a manner analogous to CV. It may also provide data that reflect a proportion of "multiracial" citizens who are not easily classified by single-member majority-minority districts. CV and related systems such as STV allow voters to define for *themselves* what aspect of their interests, ideology, beliefs, or demographic trait should be represented. If, instead of a "salad bowl," there is now a real "melting pot" in the making in the United States, then ordinal systems allow the expression of those nuances. As noted earlier, there are now more than fifty U.S. cities over 100,000 population where *at least* two ethnic or racial minorities each make up over 10 percent of residents.

As compact urban areas become more socially diverse, creating race-conscious districts in compliance with the court's new strict scrutiny standards will become increasingly difficult at any level of government. It should also be underscored that the districting process, even in the absence of overt gerrymandering, has generated a series of extremely costly and long-running legal fights. In some cases, these fights over boundary lines threaten to last longer than ten years and hence to overrun the time when a new census and even newer districts are demanded (Engstrom 2000). When all of these factors are combined, there may eventually be more widespread consideration of the electoral system alternatives discussed here.

Of course, the alternatives have been under discussion for quite some time. In a speech delivered to the U.S. Senate in July 1867, Senator Buckalew proposed the use of CV. He argued that the SMD system was unjust to (opinion) minorities, leaving many not having an elected representative to voice their (the voters') concerns. CV would give them a voice and, he argued, would bring into public life able people excluded under the current system. In addition, it would abolish gerrymandering and lessen racial and regional tensions by avoiding the racial polarization of the districted system (Buckalew 1872). With some amendments, Buckalew's commentary could well be part of modern discussions of the same topic. More modern treatments, most notably those by Guinier, would place greater emphasis on the link between minority status with race than did Buckalew, but there is nothing inherently race based about such systems. For English Victorians the relevant minorities given voice by CV were religious. In Illinois, they were regional partisan minorities. In the British Cape Colonies, they were the English settlers.

Many of these debates over the properties of different electoral systems have lasted for years. In the case of aspects of minority rights under CV, the debates have cycled and recycled for roughly 150 years. One of the things that helped these debates continue has been the absence of appropriate data. True enough, in questions of electoral reform there are often motivated biases. Those who do well under one of the current systems or who have a fondness for it for other reasons may not always be the most receptive to reform ideas. There are, as the saying has it, none so deaf as those who will not hear. But dismissing the objections to reform as mere reflections of bias really is not very satisfactory. After all, reformers have their biases too. It is not unreasonable to ask advocates of reform to offer some demonstration that the proposed alternative does, in fact, do what its proponents suggest. This requires some hard evidence on the part of those who—like Buckalew or Guinier—would claim that systems such as CV have something to offer. Up until now, however, there has been relatively little systematic empirical evidence in favor of the claims made by proponents of CV or indeed of electoral reform in general. To some extent, then, electoral reformers remained chained by a case of dueling analogies: for every pro-proportional representation (PR) reform example of Scandinavia there is an antireform analogy in the case of Italy. And whether differences between these two examples are due to institutional or cultural factors remains an open question.

Here, in gathering data on a relatively large number of cases, we have for the first time brought a relevant body of evidence to bear on these questions and on the arguments of those who would like to introduce further use of CV and LV in the United States. And we have shown that it does seem to be the case that changing the electoral systems can produce real changes in the conduct of politics at the local level. The changes are modest but measurable. More elections become competitive as more candidates enter more races, more groups work to mobilize voters, more voters turn out at the polls, and more minorities achieve electoral success. All of these seem to be solid and sustainable gains to the democratic process at the local level. Further, these gains seem to be made without many of the disadvantages that seem to be associated with redistricting on racial lines or with rigid list-PR systems.

Advantages of Ordinal, Preferential Voting in a Multicultural Polity

At several points in this book we have discussed some of the costs associated with SMDs. Given our findings at the local level, we expect that legislative districts based on race may produce muted candidate activity and lower participation than what is possible under CV. And, of course, there are the constitutional challenges to these districts, some now accepted by the courts. These districts may also produce the loss of minority "influence" over a legislature, since minority voters must be concentrated into a relatively small number of districts to ensure that some minority representatives are elected. In other (white) districts, representatives may be much less sympathetic to minority group interests.[12]

There may thus be another critical cost to districting that should increasingly be of concern to citizens and policy makers living in a society where the mix of social, ethnic, and racial interests is growing more diverse each year. One property of election laws is that some are better (or worse) at reflecting changing social circumstances and political interests. As noted, ordinal systems such as CV and STV give voters multiple options for expressing their preferences. These systems allow voters and candidates to define for themselves which interests should be promoted in the election of a representative. They also allow individuals to influence multiple candidates and thus possibly express multiple interests. Under SMD, in contrast, cartographers and the incumbent legislators who shape their maps play a huge role in predetermining which interests will be represented. Interests that are privileged by district lines and spatial segregation are thus advantaged over others.

Mansbridge (1999) and Guinier (1994) recognized the costs of privileging any particular group with static arrangements that enhance descriptive representation. Along with others (see Valadez 2001), they also noted that CV may provide a more fluid form of descriptive representation better suited for expressing constituents' multifaceted, cross-cutting interests. Descriptive representation via districting is rather rigid: boundaries rarely change more than only once every ten years, and conceptions of the groups to be preselected for descriptive representation change even less frequently. We have demonstrated that CV can change how electoral politics are conducted. It should also be stressed that CV, or STV, provides for fluidity in the process of how groups are selected for descriptive representation.

Mansbridge's normative work (1999, 652) implied strongly that the greatest cost of majority-minority districting is "essentialism"—that is,

> the assumption that members of certain groups have an essential identity that all members of that group share and of which no others can partake. Insisting that women represent women or Blacks represent Blacks, for example, implies an essential quality of womanness or Blackness that all members of that group share. Insisting that others cannot adequately represent the members of a descriptive group also implies that members of that group cannot adequately represent others. (637)

Guinier (1994) argued that one critical advantage of CV is that it moves beyond such essentialism. CV allows citizens to choose a descriptive representative exclusively, to divide votes across a descriptive representative and different representative, or to give all votes to different representatives. Since each new election allows voters and candidates to be the primary mechanism shaping descriptive representation (in contrast to the static essentialism of district cartography), we expect that results from this process may have greater legitimacy in the eyes of citizens, white and nonwhite.

Before making too strong a claim on behalf of systems such as CV, we should remind ourselves that electoral systems are just one component of the machinery of government and that this component has, in some sense, been oversold by electoral engineers. Few, perhaps, would advance the claim that if we change the electoral system we can solve all of a given society's problems, but some do make great claims on behalf of an electoral system. Yet in some cases election rules may not be the best institution for pursuing society's goals: some goals, such as minority rights, may be better pursued by courts, through education, or through civil society than by elections of any kind.

Elections and electoral systems do remain central components of any definition of a democratic system. The standard way of judging electoral arrangements is to see how well or how poorly they translate an underlying distribution of individual preferences into some social outcome. Debates within the comparative study of electoral systems over degrees of proportionality map pretty well to debates within America over descriptive representation. They both emphasize only a partial look at the problem of representative institutions: one that emphasizes just the *outcomes* and not the *process* of politics.

We know, for example, how to change the outcome of an election in some setting by changing the electoral system. We know the "levers" to pull in system design in order to privilege big parties versus small parties or vice versa. But we know less about the other kinds of consequences—those that affect how elections are contested. Different electoral institutions imply not just different winners but also different ways of winning, as well as different ways that the same people might win. We can see this especially clearly in the case of CV when candidates build electoral constituencies: they may decide to build geographically around a specific location within a district, or they may decide to try to build social constituency across the district. More than this, electoral systems can shape how much effort candidates exert in bringing people to the polls and, seemingly, whether we can find candidates willing even to stand. The previous chapters illustrate that alternative systems can have positive effects in these areas: we see that electoral institutions affect *how* people are represented and not just *if* they are.

For many years, the standard electoral engineering answer to the question of minority representation in the United States has largely been limited to one criterion, and one option: descriptive representation via SMSP districts. Practical considerations of alternatives that might also affect the vigor of campaigns, the mobilization of candidates, the mobilization of local political organizations or parties, incentives to mobilize voters, and the voter's ability to express complex preferences have been largely been ignored as ends in and of themselves. If we consider evidence from the previous chapters, it would appear that CV is a marked improvement over at-large plurality. It is reasonable to expect it could also be a substantial improvement over SMSP districting as used in the United States.

This study does not show that CV is the cure for all ills in America's body politic. But it shows that CV does have a lot to offer in making a series of improvements in civic life.

APPENDIX A.
Communities Identified as Using CV or LV

BODY	CITY	COUNTY	STATE	ELECT TYPE	YEAR ADOPTED	POP. 1990	NOT VERIF.
Dem Ex Con		Conecuh	AL	LV	1987	14,054	
Co Bd of Comm		Chilton	AL	CV	1988	32,458	
Bd of Educ		Chilton	AL	CV	1988	32,458	
City Council	Centre	Cherokee	AL	CV	1988	2,893	
City Council	Guin	Marion	AL	CV	1988	2,464	
City Council	Heath	Covington	AL	CV	1988	182	Yes
City Council	Myrtlewood	Marengo	AL	CV	1988	197	Yes
City Council	Ariton	Dale	AL	LV	1988	743	Yes
City Council	Cuba	Sumter	AL	LV		390	Yes
City Council	Dora	Walker	AL	LV	1988	2,214	
City Council	Faunsdale	Marengo	AL	LV		96	Yes
City Council	Fulton	Clarke	AL	LV	1988	384	Yes
City Council	Goshen	Pike	AL	LV		302	Yes
City Council	Kinsey	Houston	AL	LV	1988	1,679	
City Council	Loachapoka	Lee	AL	LV	1988	259	Yes
City Council	Lowndesboro	Lowndes	AL	LV	1988	139	Yes
City Council	Madrid	Houston	AL	LV	1988	211	Yes
City Council	Orrville	Dallas	AL	LV		234	Yes
City Council	Pennington	Choctow	AL	LV	1988	302	Yes
City Council	Pickensville	Pickens	AL	LV	1987	162	Yes
City Council	Pine Apple	Wilcox	AL	LV	1987	365	Yes
City Council	Providence	Marengo	AL	LV	1988	307	Yes
City Council	Rutlage	Crenshaw	AL	LV	1987	473	Yes
City Council	Silas	Choctow	AL	LV	1988	245	Yes
City Council	Toxey	Choctow	AL	LV	1988	211	Yes
City Council	Waldo	Talladega	AL	LV	1988	309	Yes
City Council	Waverly	Chambers	AL	LV	1988	152	Yes
City Council	Webb	Houston	AL	LV	1987	1,039	
City Council	Peoria	Peoria	IL	CV	1991	11,3504	
Co Bd of Comm		Bladen	NC	LV	1988	28,663	
Bd of Ed		Bladen	NC	LV	1988	28,663	
Co Bd of Comm.		Beaufort	NC	LV	1991	42,283	
Bd of Ed		Beaufort	NC	LV	1994	42,283	
Co Bd of Comm		Martin	NC	LV	1992	25,078	
Bd of Ed		Anson	TX	LV	1994	23,474	
Bd of Ed		Perguimans	NC	LV	1994	10,447	
Co Sch Dist		Perguimans	NC	LV	1994	10,447	

BODY	CITY	COUNTY	STATE	ELECT TYPE	YEAR ADOPTED	POP. 1990	NOT VERIF.
Co Sch Dist		Cleveland	NC	LV		84,714	
City Council	Robertsnvl	Martin	NC	LV	1991	1,940	
City Council	Williamson	Martin	NC	LV	1991	5,503	
City Council	Lovinton		NM	CV			Yes
City Council	Alamogordo	Otero	NM	CV	1987	27,595	
School Bd.	Sisseton		SD	CV	1991		
City Council	Abernathy	Hale & Lubbock	TX	CV	1995	2,720	
City Council	Andrews		TX	CV		10,678	
City Council	Anson	Jones	TX	CV	1996	2,644	
City Council	Anton	Hockley	TX	CV	1995	1,212	
City Council	Atlanta		TX	CV			Yes
City Council	Boerne		TX	CV			
City Council	Earth	Lamb	TX	CV	1995	1,228	
City Council	Friona	Parmer	TX	CV	1994	3,688	
City Council	Grapeland		TX	LV		1,450	
City Council	Hale Center	Hale	TX	CV	1994	2,067	
City Council	Journdntwn		TX	CV	1997	3,220	
City Council	Morton	Cochran	TX	CV	1994	2,597	
City Council	O'Donnell	Dawson	TX	CV	1996	1,102	
City Council	Olton	Lamb	TX	CV	1995	2,116	
City Council	Poth		TX	CV	1997		
City Council	Roscoe	Nolan	TX	CV	1997	1,039	
City Council	Rotan	Fisher	TX	CV	1995	1,913	
City Council	Yorktown	Dewitt	TX	CV	1992	2,207	
Ind Sch Dist	Abernathy		TX	CV	1997	3,468	
Ind Sch Dist	Amarillo		TX	CV	2000	157,000	
Ind Sch Dist	Amherst		TX	CV	1997	1,026	
Ind Sch Dist	Andrews	Andrews	TX	CV	1994	14,338	
Ind Sch Dist	Big Springs		TX	CV	1998		Yes
Ind Sch Dist	Bovina	Parmer	TX	CV	1994	5,069	
Ind Sch Dist	Denver City	Yoakum	TX	CV	1994	6,697	
nd Sch Dist	Dumas	Moore	TX	CV	1995	15,902	
Ind Sch Dist	Abernathy	Hale	TX	CV	1995	2,887	
Ind Sch Dist	Anson	Jones	TX	CV	1995	3,724	
Ind Sch Dist	Anton		TX	CV	1997	1,548	
Ind Sch Dist	Atlanta	Cass	TX	CV	1995	6,118	
Ind Sch Dist	Friona	Parmer	TX	CV	1994	4,794	
Ind Sch Dist	Hale Center	Hale	TX	CV	1994	3,139	
Ind Sch Dist	Irion County	Irion	TX	CV	1997	1,629	
Ind Sch Dist	Lockhart	Caldwell	TX	Mix	1989	14,005	
Ind Sch Dist	Luling		TX	CV		6,332	
Ind Sch Dist	Morton	Cochran	TX	CV	1994	3,569	

BODY	CITY	COUNTY	STATE	ELECT TYPE	YEAR ADOPTED	POP. 1990	NOT VERIF.
Ind Sch Dist	Navarro		TX	CV	1997	3,314	
Ind Sch Dist	O'Donnell	Dawson	TX	CV	1995	1,685	
Ind Sch Dist	Olton		TX	CV	1997	3,001	
Ind Sch Dist	Post		TX	CV	1997	4,951	
Ind Sch Dist	Poth		TX	CV	1997	3,173	
Ind Sch Dist	Riviera		TX	CV	1997	1,782	
Ind Sch Dist	Ropes		TX	CV	1997	1,300	
Ind Sch Dist	Rotan	Fischer	TX	CV	1995	2,474	
Ind Sch Dist	Springlake-Earth	Lamb	TX	CV	1995	2,035	
Ind Sch Dist	Stanford	Haskell	TX				
	Co Line	Jones	TX	CV	1995	4,146	
Ind Sch Dist	Sudan		TX	CV	1997	1,416	
Ind Sch Dist	Sundown		TX	CV	1998	1,963	
Ind Sch Dist	Wilson		TX	CV	1998	1,140	
Ind Sch Dist	Yoakum	Lavaca	TX	CV	1993	5,730	
Ind Sch Dist	Yorktown	Dewitt	TX	CV	1992	4,388	

Many of these cases were first identified by Robert Brischetto. The authors are responsible for any errors here."Yes" under "Not Verif." indicates that we are not certain as to whether a place uses an alternative election system. Alamogordo no longer uses CV.

APPENDIX B.
Candidate Survey Methods (Chapters 4, 5, and 6)

In the spring and summer of 1996 and in the spring of 1997 we surveyed a sample of most candidates who sought office in cumulative voting (CV) places between 1994 and 1997. Surveys were mailed to candidates who sought office in all U.S. places with populations over 1,000 that were identified to be using CV as of 1995. All these places are in Alabama, Illinois, Texas, New Mexico, and South Dakota. There were some candidates from smaller jurisdictions using CV in Alabama who were not surveyed. Candidate names were obtained from local officials, and addresses were obtained from officials and from database searches We referred to the 1990 U.S. Census to identify two highly similar communities near each of the jurisdictions using CV. These matching communities were selected on the basis of having ethnic/racial composition, median income, and population that closely matched the CV places. Officials were contacted for information on the electoral systems in these places.

While keeping non-election-system factors constant, we identified places using standard at-large and single-member district (SMD) elections that experienced (or were experiencing) the same Voting Rights Act (VRA) litigation and threats of litigation that caused other places to adopt CV. Many of the matched places were also undergoing VRA litigation or anticipated possible litigation. Nearly all of the matched places that switched election plans during this period ended up adopting SMD, with a few switching to mixed SMD/at-large systems. Of the places we found using SMD, most had switched in the 1990s (the same time other places adopted CV). Two of the matched places we identified that had been contesting elections under standard at-large systems were switching to CV after 1996. Non-CV cities were typically located in the same county as the CV places they were matched with. Non-CV counties and school districts were all in the same state as the CV jurisdiction they were matched with and typically were near the CV county or district. In winter and spring of 1997, we surveyed candidates who had sought office in these matched communities in 1996 and 1997.

All candidates were sent an eight-page survey asking them about their most recent campaign, with many identical questions asked of CV and non-CV candidates. Candidates were sent surveys even if their election was canceled for lack of opposition. For each wave of the survey, a multiple-contact method was used. Surveys were sent with a letter of introduction followed by a phone call. Two weeks later, postcard reminders were mailed, and another phone call was made to nonrespondents. A second copy of the survey, with a cover letter, was subsequently sent to nonrespondents. In total, 711 valid addresses were identified, and 301 surveys (42 percent) were returned. This response rate is similar to other studies of *elected* officials (e.g., Button and Hedge [1996, 34 percent and 40 percent]; Moncrief, Thompson, and Kurtz [1996, 44 percent]; Dolan and Ford [1995, 46 percent]).

Our respondents include more winners (70 percent) than losers (30 percent), but this is to be expected, since many of these places have elections that involve only a small number more candidates than seats being contested.[1] Our method produced substantial variation in the type of election system under which respondents sought office. Forty-two percent were candidates in CV elections, 30 percent ran in at-large places, and 27 percent ran in districted places.[2] Demographically our respondents closely matched the initial mailing lists. For example, the percentage of women in the candidate population was equal to the percentage of women responding (23 percent).[3] The majority of the respondents were white males, and 14 percent identified themselves as minority (either Latino/Latina/Mexican American, African American/Black, or Native American. The modal age category for respondents was 41 to 50. More candidates (46 percent) reported running for city council, with others running for county councils and school boards.

Jurisdictions where candidates were surveyed:

CV Places:

Chilton County, AL (Schools and County Board)
Guin, AL
Peoria, IL
Alamogordo, NM
Abernathy, TX
Andrews, TX
Anson, TX
Anton, TX
Bovina, TX
Denver City, TX
Dumas, TX
Earth, TX
Friona, TX
Hale Center, TX
Lockhart, TX
Morton, TX
O'Donnell, TX
Olton, TX
Rotan, TX
Yoakum, TX
Yorktown, TX

Non-CV Places

Bridgeport, AL
Carbon Hill, AL
Covington County, AL
Fulton, AL
Lawrence County, AL
McKenzie, AL
Red Level, AL
Rutledge, AL
Vernon, AL
Decatur, IL
Rockford, IL
Clovis, NM
Hobbs, NM
Flandreau, SD
Platte, SD
Aransas Pass, TX
Balmorhea, TX
Bishop, TX
Brownfield, TX
Colorado City, TX
Commerce, TX
Crosbytown, TX
Cuero, TX
Dimmitt, TX
George West, TX
Gonzales, TX
Kaufman, TX
Lockney, TX
Loraine, TX
Lorenzo, TX
Petersberg, TX
Plains, TX
Pleaseanton, TX
Post, TX*
Ralls, TX
Refugio, TX
Seagraves, TX
Stanton, TX
Sundown, TX
Three Rivers, TX
Tulia, TX

*Surveyed prior to scheduled change to CV.

APPENDIX C.
Case Selection Methods: Turnout Data (Chapter 7)

Data on turnout in local elections were requested from the largest jurisdictions in the United States that employed cumulative voting (CV) or limited voting (LV) as of 1995. Although approximately 100 jurisdictions now use CV, a number of them are very small towns. We sought turnout data only from forty-five of those CV places having a 1990 population over 1,000 persons. Of these forty-five places, we received turnout data from twenty-eight (a 62 percent response rate).

For comparison, turnout data were also obtained from a set of communities using plurality elections. The second set of cases was carefully selected so that each plurality jurisdiction closely matched a specific CV place in terms of key geographic and social characteristics. The 1990 U.S. Census was used for this purpose, allowing us to identify community-level measures of race and ethnicity, population size, percentage of residents having a high school degree, and median income. Each jurisdiction using CV was matched with a plurality jurisdiction of similar size, having similar levels of median income, high school graduates, and minority (nonwhite) population. We identified forty-five of these places and received data from twenty-one.

In model 1, data from all these places were used (elections from the twenty-eight CV places and the twenty-one matched places). Model 2 used only elections for places that had a match in the data set. Model 3 was limited to cases that were matched by place and time.

APPENDIX D. Jurisdictions Included in Turnout Analysis as Matched Places (Chapter 7): Number of Election Cases Used in Models 2 and 3, Table 7.3

		Model 2 Matched by Place		Model 3 Matched by Place and Time	
JURISDICTION	Alt Elect?	PLACE MATCH	No. of Elections	PLACE AND TIME MATCH	No. of Elections
Alamogordo, NM	Yes	Clovis, NM	6	Alamogordo, NM	2
Anton, TX, ISD	Yes	Plains, TX, ISD	5	Anson, TX, ISD	2
Anton, TX, ISD	Yes	Plains, TX, ISD	7	Anton, TX, ISD	6
Anton, TX	Yes	Plains, TX	1		
Balmorhea, TX	Yes	O'Donnell, TX	2	Balmorhea, TX	2
Boerne, TX	Yes	George West, TX	2	Boerne, TX	1
Centre, AL	Yes	Bridgeport, AL	1	Centre, AL	1
Clovis, NM	No	Alamogordo, NM	3	Clovis, NM	2
Dumas, TX, ISD	Yes	Sweetwater, TX	1	Dumas, TX, ISD	1
Earth, TX	Yes	Lorenzo, TX	6	Earth, TX	1
George West, TX	No	Boerne, TX	5	George West, TX	1
Guin, AL	Yes	Carbon Hill, AL	6	Guin, AL	2
Hale Center, TX, ISD	Yes	Lockney, TX, ISD	2	Hale Center, TX, ISD	2
Irion Co., TX, ISD	Yes	Sudan, TX, ISD	1	Irion County, TX, ISD	1
Luling, TX, ISD	Yes		4		
O'Donnell, TX, ISD	Yes	Balmorhea, TX, ISD	5	O'Donnell, TX, ISD	2
Peoria, IL	Yes	Rockford, IL	4	Peoria, IL	4
Petersburg, TX	No	Olton, TX	7	Petersburg, TX	3
Plains, TX	No	Anton, TX	5	Plains, TX	5
Post, TX, ISD	No	Anson, TX, ISD	4		
Ralls, TX	No	Morton City, TX	5	Ralls, TX	5
Refugio, TX	No	Abernathy, TX	6	Refugio, TX	3
Rockford, IL	No	Peoria, IL	6	Rockford, IL	4
Seagraves, TX, ISD	No	Abernathy, ISD	1		
Sudan, TX, ISD	No	Irion Co., TX, ISD	4	Sudan, TX, ISD	1
Sweetwater, TX, ISD	No	Dumas, TX, ISD	5	Sweetwater, TX, ISD	1
Yorktown, TX, ISD	Yes		6	Yorktown, TX, ISD	2
Bridgeport, AL	No	Centre, AL	1	Bridgeport, AL	1
Lorenzo, TX	No	Earth, TX	1	Lorenzo, TX	1
Anton, TX	Yes	Plains, TX	9	Anton, TX	1
Lorenzo TX	No	Earth, TX	2		
Abernathy, TX	Yes	Refugio, TX	6	Abernathy, TX	3
Carbon Hill, AL	No	Guin, AL	3	Carbon Hill, AL	2
Lockney, TX	No	Hale Center, TX	7	Lockney, TX	2

JURISDICTION	Alt Elect?	Model 2 Matched by Place: PLACE MATCH	Model 2 Matched by Place: No. of Elections	Model 3 Matched by Place and Time: PLACE AND TIME MATCH	Model 3 Matched by Place and Time: No. of Elections
Lorenzo, TX	No		1		
Morton, TX	Yes	Ralls, TX	8	Morton, TX	5
Plains, TX, ISD	No	Anton, TX, ISD	6	Plains, TX, ISD	6
Olton, TX	Yes	Petersberg, TX	6	Olton, TX	3
Roscoe, TX	Yes	Sundown, TX	5	Roscoe, TX	4
Sundown, TX	No	Roscoe, TX	5	Sundown, TX	4

*Data prior to scheduled shift to CV.

APPENDIX E.
Case Selection Methods: Election Result Data (Chapter 8)

This analysis is limited to jurisdictions for which 1990 census population data are available. Information on local election systems and election results were obtained in the spring of 1995 via telephone interviews with city clerks and county election officials, with additional data acquired in subsequent interviews in 1996, 1997, and 1998. Given different response rates in each phase of our study, we do not have perfect overlap between these cases and those examined considered in chapter 7, and those assessed here. These are most of the same jurisdictions that our candidate survey was conducted in.

APPENDIX F.
Jurisdictions Included in the Population-Seats Analysis (Models 1 and 2, Chapter 8)

MODEL 1		MODEL 2		MODELS 8–10	
ALL PLACES	NO. OF ELECTIONS	BLACK PLACES	NO. OF ELECTIONS	LATINO PLACES W/ TURNOUT DATA	
Chilton	2	Chilton	2		
Centre	2	Centre	2		
Guin	3	Guin	3		
Myrtlewood	1	Myrtlewood	1		
Dora	2	Dora	2		
Kinsey	1	Kinsey	1		
Webb	2	Webb	2		
Peoria	2	Peoria	2		
Bladen	3	Bladen	3		
Beaufort	3	Beaufort	3		
Martin	2	Martin	2		
Anson	2	Anson	2		
Perguimans	1	Perguimans	1		
Jamesville	1	Jamesville	1		
Alamogordo	3				
Sisseton	2				
Abernathy	1				
Andrews	1				
Anton	2			Anton	1
Atlanta	1	Atlanta	1	Atlanta	1
Boerne	1				
Earth	2			Earth	1
Friona	2			Friona	1
Grapeland	1	Grapeland	1		
Hale Center	3				
Jordonton	1				
Morton	3			Morton	1
Olton	2			Olton	1
Poth	1				
Roscoe	1			Roscoe	1
Rotan	2			Rotan	1
Yorktown	1				

MODEL 1		MODEL 2		MODELS 8–10	
ALL PLACES	NO. OF ELECTIONS	BLACK PLACES	NO. OF ELECTIONS	LATINO PLACES W/ TURNOUT DATA	
Abernathy	2				
Amherst	1				
Andrews	1			Andrews	1
Anson	2				
Anton	1				
Bovina	3				
Denver City	3			Denver City	1
Dumas	2				
Dumas	1				
Friona	3			Friona	1
Hale Center	3				
Irion County	1				
Lockhart	3				
Luling	1				
Morton	3			Morton	1
Navarro	1				
O'Donnell	1				
Olton	1				
Post	1				
Poth	1				
Riviera	1				
Ropes	1				
Rotan	2			Rotan	1
Springlake-Earth	2				
Stamford County[1]	1			Stamford	1
Sudan	1				
Sundown	1				
Wilson	1				
Yoakum	3				
Yorktown	3			Yorktown	1
Sisseton	2				
Chilton	3	Chilton	3		
Total cases	118		32		15

NOTES

Notes to Chapter 1

1. According to the 1990 census, 15.3 percent of residents were Hispanic, 6.1 percent were African American, and 2.6 percent were "other."
2. In addition to the change in election system between 1998 and 2000, there was a referendum on the 2000 ballot that may have affected turnout. As we see in chapter 7, however, there is a systematic increase in turnout associated with the adoption of CV, but it is only about half as large as the turnout increase that occurred in Amarillo.
3. The U.S. Census recorded race and Hispanic-origin data for 419,716 of the 493,830 county, city, town, school district, and special-district elected officials in the United States in 1992 (Department of Commerce, 1999).
4. As of 1987, there were 38,933 municipalities, townships, and counties in the United States (Burns 1994).
5. *Thornburg v. Gingles,* 478 US 30 (June 30, 1986).
6. *Shaw v. Reno,* 113 SCt 2816 (1993).
7. CV is classified as an ordinal system, since it allows voters the ability to express multiple preferences in a ranked order. The single transferable vote (STV), used in Australia, Ireland, and Malta, is another ordinal system.
8. For example, the set of Scandinavian countries share a broadly similar set of PR-based institutional arrangements as well as common cultural and social traits. Likewise, the Anglophone democracies have shared traditions and histories that lead them to share a set of majoritarian institutions.
9. One notable exception is the considerable body of work concerning Duverger's Law and the related phenomenon of tactical voting in single-member, simple-plurality (SMSP) systems (e.g., Black 1978). Some of the most sophisticated individual-level analysis can be seen in the series of papers by Franklin, Niemi, and Whitten (1992) and Niemi, Whitten, and Franklin (1992) and attendant debates.
10. In general, it seems easier to achieve finer divisions into integers of a larger number than a smaller one; hence, there are more proportional election results when there are more seats to be allocated per district.
11. As Lord Boothby reportedly said, "Ideally the House of Commons should be a social microcosm of the nation. The nation includes a great many people who are rather stupid, and so should the House" (quoted in Birch 1971, 59).

Notes to Chapter 2

1. STV is used to elect multiple candidates to a legislature. Voters rank-order their preferred candidates when voting. A formula that includes the number of seats and number of voters is used to determine how many votes (the quota) are needed to win a seat. In the first round of counting votes, any candidate reaching the quota is declared elected. Surplus votes from that candidate can transfer to other candidates having less than a quota in subsequent rounds of counting votes.
2. *Allen v. Alabama State Board of Education,* 164 F3d 136 (1969).
3. The purpose of the original Section 2 was to enforce the Fifteenth Amendment's prohibition against denial of voting on the basis of race by declaring that a violation of Section 2 would be evaluated on the "totality of circumstances" associated with participation. Section 2 also states that "nothing in this section establishes a right to have members of a protected class elected in numbers equal to their proportion in the population."
4. This problem of at-large elections is not restricted to race politics. In the southern California town of Hemet, a large concentration of retirees can dominate school board elections, no matter what outlying communities of parents wish.
5. Alternatively, descriptive representation might empower minority residents of these districts with greater efficacy, encouraging them to participate.
6. *Shaw v. Reno,* 113 SCt 2816 (1993).
7. *Miller v. Johnson,* 515 US 900, 916 (1995).
8. *Shaw v. Hunt,* 116 SCt 1895, 1905 (1996); *Bush v. Vera,* 116 SCt 1941, 1956–58 (1996).
9. As a historical note, this passage predates the 1854 letter by James Garth Marshall to Lord Russell. But it has proved difficult to uncover the identity of the person who wrote the passage. The report itself is signed by the secretary to the Privy Council, William Bathurst. Marshall does not seem to be a member of the Privy Council. Note also the comments of Fairbairn, a member of the then advisory Cape Legislative Council in September 1850 (Parliamentary Papers, 1851, vol. 38, p. 207).
10. *Reno v. Bossier Parish School Board,* 520 US 471 (1997).
11. The fact that this statement comes from high-ranking politicians in imperial Britain more than a century before the U.S. Voting Rights Act does seem somewhat surprising. It was certainly something of a surprise to the governor of the Cape Colony, who was expecting to be told to set up an appointed, not an elected, upper house.
12. No nonwhite member was elected, but non-Europeans did represent a sizable portion of the electorate wooed by candidates. In 1892 Ahmed Effendi, a Moslem, stood as a candidate in Cape Town. He was not elected in part

due to the "speedy abolition of the cumulative vote in Cape Town" (McCracken 1967, 75). If nothing else, his candidacy and the reaction to it suggest the power of CV to help minority groups.

13. The 1870 school board elections were the first elections in which women could vote. And, in fact, the 1870 election saw the election of a woman candidate—Dr. Garrett—by a landslide.
14. As we show, CV has worked well to produce minority representation in these places. In Sisseton, however, Native Americans, while initially succesful in winning seats, have not been elected in elections held since the jursidiction was expanded to include more white voters.
15. In Texas, Rolando Rios has advocated CV with LULAC; In Alabama, Ed Still and Jerome Gray of the Alabama Democratic Conference promoted LV. Mike Crowell played a similar role in North Carolina.
16. Illinois allowed half-votes.
17. This oddly neglected paper by Grofman also provides thresholds of representation and exclusion for a variety of other electoral systems.
18. The tricky aspect of list PR is that vote shares are rarely neat numbers. It is rarely the case, for example, that there is a 100-seat legislature where four parties receive vote percentages that are exact integers (e.g., exactly 25 percent of the vote each). The Norwegian Storting, for example, has 165 seats. The 1997 election saw ten different party groups running, gaining untidy vote totals such as 0.6 percent (Pensioner's Party) and 13.7 percent (Christian Democrats). There are several different ways of dealing with these awkward leftover fractions of vote shares. Each of these methods has different consequences: some benefit larger parties, others smaller ones.
19. Some "open" list-PR systems, most notably Finland's, do allow some choice of candidates, but these exceptions are rare (Farrell 2001).
20. Another attempt to find a middle ground is sometimes found in use of a type of "mixed" system based in varying degrees of looseness on the German model. This mixed model essentially combines list PR and SMSP at the same time and gives voters two votes—one under each system, one of which is for a party list and the other of which is for a candidate. Russia, Mexico, Scotland, Wales, and New Zealand all have systems of this kind. These mixed systems weigh and combine the two different votes in varying ways: in some places the "districts" are national, other places they are not (see Farrell 2001; Shugart and Wattenberg 2001).

Notes to Chapter 3

1. Little wonder, too, that formal treatments interested in minority representation tend to assume an equal distribution of votes among candidates in order to make the problem tractable.
2. As Wiggins and Petty (1979) illustrated, these arrangements did not necessarily cause Illinois elections to be less competitive.
3. Similar problems are posed in other systems Skill at nomination strategies has been cited as an explanation for the seat bonuses received by Japan's Liberal Democratic Party (LDP) under a form of limited voting (Cox and Niou 1994). Other examples include nomination and vote management strategies under the single transferable vote system (STV) (see the examples in Bowler and Grofman 2000).
4. *Gomez v. City of Watsonville,* 863 F2d 1407, 1414 (9th Cir. 1988); *Garza v. County of Los Angeles,* 918 F2d 763, 770–771 (9th Cir. 1990).
5. Take, for example, the following exchange from an 1884 parliamentary hearing on CV:

    Mr. Courtney: If a party ran too many candidates it might not gain its due proportion of power.

    Mr. Sanford: Quite so. That is its own fault. (Parliament 1884–85, 78)
6. We classify CV as an ordinal plan because it allows voters the opportunity to give some candidates more support than others when they vote. However, CV and LV do not force voters to rank-order preferences, as is the case with the STV and alternative vote (AV) systems.

Notes to Chapter 4

1. We illustrate this with Morton, Texas, ISD and Peoria, Illinois, council elections, since these are two of the CV cases where we have the longest time series of election data.
2. Interestingly, only 12 percent acknowledge that groups worked on their own behalf to tell voters how to divide their votes. This difference could be a result of who our respondents were.
3. Pildes and Donoghue (1995) also suggest that some (white?) candidates adopted geographic vote apportionment strategies similar to those adopted by larger parties in Victorian England, where they focused their appeals for votes on a specific sections of the county
4. These included such activities as knocking on doors, walking precincts, public speaking, writing letters, telephoning voters, organizing events, and purchasing ads.

Notes to Chapter 5

Part of this chapter was written with Tracy Sulkin.

1. More elaborate OLS regression models not reported here also fail to demonstrate any differences in frequency of activities across systems. The models included as control variables a dummy indicator distinguishing between large and small places, a dummy that identified incumbents, a dummy that identified minority candidates, and a dummy indicating that the candidate was opposed.
2. With the first two waves of our survey, we were able to match survey returns with information from local officials in order to ascertain if a candidate ran unopposed. In the final waves of the survey, this information was not available. This means that the samples in tables 5.1 and 5.2 do not overlap perfectly. Many of these unopposed candidates nevertheless claimed to have campaigned, even though their elections might have been canceled or rendered moot due to lack of opposition. If we simply compare CV candidates to non-CV candidates on a question that asks, "Did you conduct any campaigning at all?" there is no difference between CV and non-CV candidates (chi square = 0.17, $p < .896$).
3. We should note that other writers do focus on the virtues of high expenditure and suggest that there are conditions that make campaign spending beneficial for democracy, particularly when voters have little information for making choices (Palda 1994; Lupia and Gerber 1995). From this latter perspective, campaign spending, particularly in a competitive election, represents a net information gain for voters. Less spending could therefore mean that voters would have less information about the candidates who would be their potential representatives.
4. We used a dummy variable that distinguished between candidates from small (population less than 30,000) and large (population greater than 30,000) jurisdictions in the estimates reported here. The larger communities were in New Mexico and Illinois. Other estimates using raw population (log transformed) were also significant. The dummy variable results are reported for ease of interpretation.
5. Spending for all respondents averaged only $691 (s.d. $2,061). Of candidates who did spend money (about 65 percent of all respondents), the average was $1,422, with the highest being $17,000. Given this non-normal distribution, we also estimated these models with various transformations of spending and found no substantive differences in our results. It is worth noting that a simple bivariate analysis of spending by electoral system produces the following means and standard deviations: CV, $600, $1,515; SMD, $784, $1,710; At large, $867, $3,531.
6. Other things being equal, this difference in campaign style might lead to

voters in CV communities being generally better informed, even while more candidates run. We suggest that this could lead to long-term improvements in civic life in these CV communities, including greater levels of political knowledge and information, if not greater interest and participation in politics. These issues are beyond the scope of this book, however.

7. A logistic regression equation (not shown) found that this effect held when we controlled for the variables listed in table 5.3.
8. Twenty-one percent of white candidates reported working to register voters, while 51 percent of minority candidates did (chi-square = 14.15, $p < .0001$).
9. Indeed, this might be one reason why candidates running for districted seats are less likely to be challenged.

Notes to Chapter 6

1. See Vowles et al. (1998) for extensive treatment of this problem in relation to discussion of New Zealand's change in electoral rules.
2. Little wonder, too, that formal treatments interested in minority representation tend to assume an equal distribution of votes among candidates in order to make the problem tractable.
3. Exploring this possibility has formed the basis for a small, but growing, body of work on elections in Canada and Britain where such behavior can be found. And, in general, this work shows that voters are capable of recognizing and responding to these "tactical voting" situations (Alvarez and Nagler 2000; Black 1978; Cain 1978; Lanoue and Bowler 1992; Niemi, Whitten, and Franklin 1991; Tsebelis 1986). But most of the time first-past-the-post does not invoke the need for voters to think very much beyond voting a sincere expression of a single preference.
4. We are grateful to Richard Engstrom for providing us with these data. Any error in interpretation of the data is our responsibility.
5. Two Native American candidates filed to run, but one withdrew before the election (Engstrom and Barrilleaux 1991).
6. Since it is unlikely to reflect lower education levels or lower socioeconomic status, Anglo sentiment could reflect majority hostility to elections that produce minority representation and/or the greater difficulties that majority voters and candidate face in coordinating vote dispersion across a number of candidates.

Notes to Chapter 7

1. Guinier (1994) argued that CV places a focus not on geographical representation but on interest representation (see also Still 1984; Guinier 1995).

2. This same idea also may be found in standard discussion of turnout in terms of $p * b - c$ due to Riker's (1982) discussion: having very similar candidates reduces the benefit from voting, since voters get roughly similar outcomes whoever wins.
3. Furthermore, the vast majority of elections follow the municipal model of holding elections in the off-year and in odd months. For example, all Texas city council and Independent School District (ISD) elections included in this analysis are held in early May of each year. Guin, Alabama, which does hold their elections every four years corresponding with presidential elections, does so in August, not November. There are no elections in this analysis, to our knowledge, that correspond with a national or statewide general election. The practical implication of this is that there are no national or statewide influences on turnout in these data.
4. Although most jurisdictions would provide names of winning candidates in phone interviews, some resisted providing information on turnout over the phone or via mail or fax. Refusals were greater when data from older elections were requested. Thus, from some places, we have longer time series than others.
5. For example, case 1 = $election_{ij,}$ where $_i$ is an individual election year and $_j$ is the jurisdiction.
6. Fifty-four of these were conducted under at-large rules, while 18 were conducted under districted elections.
7. *T* tests can be used to assess the significance of pairwise differences between multiple means included in an ANOVA. The tests are most appropriate when used with pairwise comparisons that are planned a priori (as is the case here). We also calculated Tukey's "honestly significant difference" (or HSD), a more conservative test designed for post hoc assessments of pairwise differences. Using the HSD measure, differences in turnout would be significant only if greater than 5 percent. Following Kirk (1995) and Evans (1996), we report the *t*-test results.
8. Given the nature these data, all communities had a sizable minority population. However, no jurisdictions had a large Latino and African American population simultaneously. The dummy variable thus equaled 1 (Latino the largest minority) or 0 (African American the largest). The majority of elections (86 percent) were contested where Latinos were the predominant minority group.
9. Likewise, aggregate levels of education could also affect participation. Our measures of income and education, however, are highly correlated (.80), and both are strongly correlated with population (each over .65). To avoid problems of multicollinearity, we omitted the measure of education. When

education was substituted for income, the substantive results did not change.

10. Since time series for places vary in length, cases are lost when the estimation is limited to instances where time of election and place are both matched.
11. The size and significance of the effect of election system reported in each estimate in table 2 remain largely unchanged when dummy variables for year are included in the models.
12. The dependent variable (turnout) has a mean of .19 and a standard deviation of .14. It ranges from .017 to .682. The distribution has a noticeable but not severe right tail, with only one case lying further than three standard deviations from the mean.
13. In these latter estimates, there is simply less variance in most independent variables.
14. Where data for at least three time points were available, we used data from the last election under plurality rules and the first two under CV/LV. Since most of our cases were from Texas, these elections were held one year apart. If only two time points were available, we used the last election under plurality and the first under CV/LV.
15. In these communities, all places switched from plurality voting to CV. There were no cases with large Latino populations switching to LV.
16. The size and significance of the effect of election system reported in each estimate in table 7.3 remain largely unchanged when dummy variables for year are included in the models.

Notes to Chapter 8

1. Strategic action by minorities in primaries may be needed more when these districts are not homogeneous, as is the case with many majority-minority districts.
2. Within individual jurisdictions, scholars and expert witnesses in Voting Rights Act (VRA) litigation can rely on precinct-level measures to correlate the racial composition of an area with votes for particular candidates. This method does not allow for cross-jurisdictional tests of the effects of election system rules on representation.
3. Given different response rates in each phase of our study, we do not have perfect overlap between the CV cases considered in chapter 7 and those assessed here.
4. For example, if a place were electing five seats via CV (or LV) in an election, the dependent variable would be calculated as the number of CV seats won by minority candidates divided by 5. Likewise, if a place elected three

seats via districts and two via CV, the dependent variable would be number of CV seats won by minority candidates divided by 2.

5. In a single CV jurisdiction (Sisseton, South Dakota, school district), the predominate minority group is Native American.
6. Like the cases in our study, then, many of these places had recently moved away from at-large plans in response to actual or potential VRA action under Section 2. As with our study, Bullock's cases were limited to places where African Americans were in the minority (n = 149 counties). Given the recent elections system changes in many of these places, and the small population and rural nature of many, we suggest that they are a good basis for making comparisons with our study.
7. Differences between our estimates from CV/LV and Bullock's estimates from at-large and SMD systems are even more striking when we consider that our models use percent minority voting-age population as the key independent variable, while Bullock uses percent minority voter registration. Given the gap between population and voter registration, our estimates could have been expected be biased against finding proportionate relationships that would be evident when registration data were used.
8. All of the variation in election plans occurred across African American places.
9. A t test of the difference between these slopes produces no significant difference. When an interaction term (LV * Minority Percent Voting-Age Population) was included with all 28 cases from table 8.3, the coefficient was positive (b = .52) but not significant.
10. The only year that turnout data by ethnic group were available for Texas places using CV was 1995. Latino candidates sought office in fifteen Texas CV elections that year, and registration data were reported for fourteen of these places. We were thus unable to prepare similar estimates using all 118 cases. These data are available in Brischetto and Engstrom (1997).

Notes to Chapter 9

Part of this chapter was written with Jeff Karp and Susan Banducci.

1. We leave to others the question of how large a group should have to be to make such a claim to representation.
2. Vanderleeuw and Utter (1993) found similar results in New Orleans, and Lublin and Voss (2000) found higher aggregate turnout when African American mayoral candidates sought office in a study on a large set of cities.
3. Response rates for the ANES for the 1990, 1992, 1994, and 1996 studies are 71 percent, 71 percent, 74 percent, and 71 percent, respectively. Each contains a "fresh" cross section and panelists from previous studies. We include

only those cases that are "fresh" in each cross section and avoid double-counting respondents. Panel analysis is not possible, as too few minority respondents are reinterviewed in the panel phases.

4. The number of Hispanics in majority-minority districts in the data set were too small to permit analysis.
5. Each cross section was merged with data on the race of the respondent's House member at the time of the survey.
6. Gilliam and Kaufman (1996) presented data suggesting that the "life cycle" for empowerment effects may last as long as twenty years in some jurisdictions.
7. We also found no evidence of white reaction to the presence of nonwhite representatives.
8. In the 1991 Peoria election, no winning white or black candidate received more than 38 percent of support from voters who plumped for a single candidate, suggesting cross-racial voting. In the Sisseton example, in contrast, the exit poll found that only 9 percent of Native Americans voted for a white candidate.
9. And for notable examples of previous work in this vein, see Brischetto and Engstrom (1997), Pildes and Donoghue (1995), Amy (1993), Engstrom (1993), Rule and Zimmerman (1992), Guinier (1991, 1998), and Still (1984).
10. Nearly all other adoptions of CV and LV resulted from consent decrees rather than orders from the bench. In 1998, however, the U.S. District Court for the Northern District of Illinois ordered a seven-member council (in Chicago Heights) elected by CV. That ruling was appealed to the U.S. Court of Appeals for the Seventh Circuit. The order has been remanded by the Circuit Court for a hearing. In 1995, a U.S. District Court in Maryland ordered CV elections for the Worchester County Commission. That ruling was latter overturned by the U.S. Court of Appeals for the Fourth Circuit. CV was also ordered by the bench for judicial election in Hamilton County, Tennessee, but the order was reversed by the Sixth Circuit.
11. Instant runoff, or the alternative vote (AV), could be used in single-member districts. Rank-ordered votes for several candidates are counted. If no one has a majority of first-preference votes on the first count, then second-preference votes from the last-placed candidate are transferred to remaining candidates until one receives a majority. STV is a rank-ordered system used in multimember districts.
12. See Grofman and Handley (1989), Lublin (1997), Swain (1993), Overby and Cosgrove (1996), Cameron, Epstein, and O'Halloran (1996), Bullock (1994), and Thernstrom (1987) for detailed discussions of the trade-off between substantive and descriptive representation.

Notes to Appendix B

1. For example, 62 percent of nonincumbents who responded won their election.
2. The response rate was slightly higher for non-CV candidates, but more CV candidates were identified in the earlier study, so there are more of them in this sample. Candidates who sought office in places using mixed systems were included as CV, at large, or SMD on the basis of the particular seat they sought most recently.
3. This is estimated by counting "female" first names of candidates and thus is not exact.

BIBLIOGRAPHY

Abramson, Paul, and John Aldrich. 1982. "The Decline of Electoral Participation in America." *American Political Science Review* 76: 502–21.

Adrian, Charles. 1952. "Some General Characteristics of Nonpartisan Elections." *American Political Science Review* 46: 766–76.

Alford, Robert, and Eugene Lee. 1968. "Voting Turnout in American Cities." *American Political Science Review* 62: 796–813.

Allen v. Alabama State Board of Education, 164 F.3d 134 (1969).

"Alternative Voting Systems as Remedies for Unlawful At-Large Systems." 1982. *Yale Law Journal* 92: 144–60.

Alvarez, Michael, and Tara Butterfield. 2000. "The Resurgence of Nativism in California? The Case of Proposition 187 and Illegal Immigration." *Social Science Quarterly* 81, no. 1 (March): 167–79.

Alvarez, Michael, and Jonathan Nagler. 2000. "A New Approach for Modeling Strategic Voting in Multiparty Elections." *British Journal of Political Science* 30, no. 1: 57–75.

Ames, B. 1995. "Electoral Strategy under Open-List Proportional Representation." *American Journal of Political Science* 39: 406–33.

Amy, Douglas. 1993. *Real Choices, New Voices.* New York: Columbia University Press.

Anderson, Christopher J., and Chris A. Guillory. 1997. "Political Institutions and Satisfaction with Democracy: A Cross-National Analysis of Consensus and Majoritarian Systems." *American Political Science Review* 91: 66–81.

Aspin, L., and W. Hall. 1996. "Cumulative Voting and Minority Candidates: An Analysis of the 1991 Peoria Elections." *American Review of Politics* 17: 225–44.

Austen-Smith, D., and J. Banks. 1988. "Elections Coalitions and Legislative Outcomes." *American Political Science Review* 82: 405–22.

Australian Election Study. 1998. Australian National Election Study Poll. Australian National University, Canberra, Australia.

Australian Electoral Commission Statistics: Result of Count (various years).

Banducci, Susan. 1999. "Proportional Representation and Attitudes about Politics: Results from New Zealand." *Electoral Studies* 18: 533–55.

Barber, Benjamin. 1984. *Strong Democracy: Participatory Politics for a New Age.* Berkeley: University of California Press.

Barber, Kathleen. 1995. *Proportional Representation and Election Reform in Ohio.* Columbus: Ohio State University Press.

———. 2000. *A Right to Representation: Proportional Election Systems for the Twenty-First Century.* Columbus: Ohio State University Press.

Bean, Clive. 1990. "The Personal Vote in Australian Federal Elections." *Political Studies* 38: 253–68.

Birch, A. H. 1971. *Representation.* London: Pall Mall Press.

Black, J. 1978. "The Multicandidate Calculus of Voting: Applications to Canadian Federal Elections." *American Journal of Political Science* 22: 609–38.

Blair, G. 1958. "Cumulative Voting: Patterns of Party Allegiance and Rational Choice in Illinois State Legislative Contests." *American Political Science Review* 52: 123–30.

Blais, André, and R. K. Carty. 1990. "Does Proportional Representation Foster Voter Turnout?" *European Journal of Politics* 18: 167–81.

Blais, André, and Agnieszka Dobrzynska. 1998. "Turnout in Electoral Democracies." *European Journal of Political Research* 33: 239–61.

Bobo, Lawrence, and Frank Gilliam. 1990. "Race, Sociopolitical Participation, and Black Empowerment." *American Political Science Review* 84: 377–97.

Bowler, Shaun. 1996. "Reasoning Voters, Voting Behavior and Institutions." In *British Elections and Parties Yearbook,* edited by D. Farrell, D. Broughton, D. Denver, and J. Fisher. London: Frank Cass.

Bowler, Shaun, David Brockington, and Todd Donovan. 1996. "Candidate Activities, Strategies and Organization in U.S. Cumulative Voting Elections." Paper presented at the American Political Science Association, San Francisco, August–September.

Bowler, Shaun, Todd Donovan, and David Brockington. 1995. "Minority Representation under Cumulative and Limited Voting." Presented at the American Political Science Association, Chicago.

Bowler, Shaun, T. Donovan, and D. Farrell. 1999. "Party Strategy and Voter Organization under Cumulative Voting in Victorian England." *Political Studies* 47, no. 5 (December): 906–17.

Bowler, Shaun, and David Farrell. 1993. "Legislator Shirking and Voter Monitoring: Impacts of European Parliament Electoral Systems upon Legislator/Voter Relationships." *Journal of Common Market Studies* 31, no. 1 (March): 45–69.

Bowler, Shaun, D. Farrell, and Ian McAllister. 1996. "Constituency Campaigning in Parliamentary Systems with Preferential Voting: Is There a Paradox?" *Electoral Studies* 15, no. 4: 461–76.

Bowler, Shaun, and B. Grofman. 2000. "Introduction." In *Elections in Australia, Ireland and Malta under the Single Transferable Vote: Reflections on an Embedded Institution,* edited by S. Bowler and B. Grofman. Ann Arbor: University of Michigan Press.

Brace, K., B. Grofman, L. Handley, and R. Niemi. 1988. "Minority Voting

Equality: The 65 Percent Rule in Theory and Practice." *Law and Policy* 10: 43–62.

Brace, Kimball, L. Handley, R. Niemi, and H. Stanley. 1995. "Minority Turnout and the Creation of Majority-Minority Districts." *American Politics Quarterly* 23: 190–203.

Brams, Steven. 1975. *Game Theory and Politics.* New York: Free Press.

Bridges, Amy. 1997. *Morning Glories: Municipal Reform in the Southwest.* Princeton, N.J.: Princeton University Press.

Brischetto, Robert. 1995. "The Rise of Cumulative Voting." *Texas Observer,* July 28, p. 6.

Brischetto, Robert, and Richard Engstrom. 1997. "Cumulative Voting and Latino Representation: Exit Surveys in Fifteen Texas Communities." *Social Science Quarterly* 78: 973–91.

Brockington, D., T. Donovan, S. Bowler, and R. Brischetto. 1998. "Minority Representation under Cumulative and Limited Voting in the U.S." *Journal of Politics* 60, no. 4: 1108–25.

Buckalew, Charles. 1872. *Proportional Representation, or the Representation of Successive Majorities in Federal, State, Municipal, Corporate and Primary Elections.* Philadelphia: Campbell and Sons.

Bullock, C. 1994. "Section 2 of the Voting Rights Act, Districting Formats and the Election of African Americans." *Journal of Politics* 56: 1098–1105.

Bullock, C., and S. MacManus. 1993. "Testing the Assumptions of the Totality of Circumstances Test." *American Politics Quarterly* 21: 290–306.

Burnham, Walter Dean. 1970. *Critical Elections and the Mainsprings of American Politics.* New York: W. W. Norton.

Burns, Nancy. 1994. *The Formation of American Local Governments: Private Values in Public Institutions.* New York: Oxford University Press.

Bush v. Vera, 116 SCt 1941, 1956–58 (1996).

Button, James, and David Hedge. 1996. "Legislative Life in the 1990s: A Comparison of Black and White State Legislators." *Legislative Studies Quarterly* 21: 199–218.

Cain, Bruce. 1978. Strategic Voting in Britain. *American Journal of Political Science* 22: 639–55.

Cain, Bruce, John Ferejohn, and Morris Fiorina. 1984. "The Constituency Basis of the Personal Vote for U.S. Representatives and British Members of Parliament." *American Political Science Review* 78: 110–25.

Cairns, Alan. 1968. "The Electoral System and the Party System in Canada: 1921–1965." *Canadian Journal of Political Science* 1: 55–80.

Caldeira, Gregory, Samuel Patterson, and Gregory Markko. 1985. "The Mobilization of Voters in Congressional Elections." *Journal of Politics* 47: 490–509.

Cameron, Charles, David Epstein, and Sharyn O'Halloran. 1996. "Do Majority-Minority Districts Maximize Substantive Black Representation in Congress?" *The American Political Science Review* 90, no. 4. (December): 794–812.

Campbell, Angus, Philip Converse, Warren Miller, and Donald Stokes. 1960. *The American Voter.* Chicago: University of Chicago Press.

Carey, John, and Matthew Soberg Shugart. 1995. "Incentives to Cultivate a Personal Vote: A Rank Ordering of Electoral Formulas." *Electoral Studies* 14: 417–39.

Center for Voting and Democracy (CVD). 1999. "Oral History Project on Illinois' Use of Cumulative Voting." Illinois Citizens for Proportional Representation/Center for Voting and Democracy, Washington, D.C.

———. 2000. "Year End Report." Center for Voting and Democracy. Washington, D.C.

Christensen, R., and P. Johnson. 1995. "Toward a Context Rich Analysis of Electoral Systems." *American Journal of Political Science* 39: 575–98.

Cohan, A. S., R. D. McKinlay, and A. Mughan. 1975. "The Used Vote and Electoral Outcomes: the Irish General Election of 1973." *British Journal of Political Science* 5: 363–83.

Cole, R., and D. Taebel. 1992. "Cumulative Voting in Local Elections: Lessons from the Alamogordo Experience." *Social Science Quarterly* 73: 194–201.

Cole, R., D. Taebel, and R. Engstrom. 1990. "Cumulative Voting in a Municipal Election: A Note on Voter Reactions and Electoral Consequences." *Western Political Quarterly* 43: 191–99.

Conway, M. Margaret. 1992. "Creative Multimember Redistricting and Representation of Women and Minorities in the Maryland Legislature." In *United States Electoral Systems: Their Impact on Women and Minorities,* edited by Wilma Rule and Joseph Zimmerman. New York: Greenwood Press.

Cox, Gary. 1990. "Centripetal and Centrifugal Incentives in Electoral Systems." *American Journal of Political Science* 34: 903–35.

———. 1991. "SNTV and d'Hondt are 'Equivalent.'" *Electoral Studies* 10: 118–32.

———. 1996. "Is the SNTV Super-Proportional? Evidence from Japan and Taiwan." *American Journal of Political Science* 40: 740–55.

———. 1997. *Making Votes Count.* New York: Cambridge University Press.

Cox, Gary, and Michael Munger. 1989. "Closeness, Expenditure and Turnout in the 1982 U.S. House Elections." *American Political Science Review* 83: 217–31.

Cox, Gary, and E. Niou. 1994. "Seats Bonuses under Single Non Transferable Vote Systems." *Comparative Political Studies* 26: 221–36.

Cox, Gary, and F. Rosenbluth. 1994. "Reducing Nomination Errors: Factional Competition and Party Strategy in Japan." *Electoral Studies* 13:4–16.

Davidson, Chandler. 1994. "The Recent Evolution of Voting Rights Law Affecting Racial and Language Minorities." In *Quiet Revolution in the South: The Impact of the Voting Rights Act 1965–1990,* edited by C. Davidson and B. Grofman. Princeton, N.J.: Princeton University Press.

Davidson, Chandler, and Luis Fraga. 1988. "Slating Groups as Parties in a 'Nonpartisan' Setting." *Western Political Quarterly* 41, no. 2: 373–90.

Davidson, Chandler, and B. Grofman. 1994. *Quiet Revolution in the South: The Impact of the Voting Rights Act 1965–1990.* Princeton, N.J.: Princeton University Press.

Davidson, Chandler, and George Korbel. 1981. "At-Large Elections and Minority Group Representation: A Reexamination of Historical and Contemporary Evidence." *Journal of Politics* 43: 982–1005.

Dodgson, C. 1884. *The Principles of Parliamentary Representation.* London: Harrison and Sons.

Dolan, Kathleen, and Lynne Ford. 1995. "Women in the State Legislature: Feminist Identity and Legislative Behaviors." *American Politics Quarterly* 23: 96–108.

Donovan, Mark. 1995. "The Politics of Electoral Reform in Italy." *International Political Science Review* 16: 47–64.

Donovan, Todd. 1993. "Community Controversy and the Adoption of Economic Development Policies." *Social Science Quarterly* 74: 386–402.

______. 2001. "Mobilization and Support of Minor Parties: Australian Senate Elections, 1922–1998." *Party Politics* 6, no. 4: 473–86.

Donovan, Todd, T. Sulkin, S. Bowler, and D. Brockington. 1997. "Contested Local Elections and Active Campaigns." Paper presented at the annual meeting of the American Political Science Association, San Francisco, California, August 31–September 2.

Downs, Anthony. 1957. *An Economic Theory of Democracy.* New York: Harper and Row.

Dunn, Charles. 1972. "Cumulative Voting: Problems in Illinois Legislative Elections." *Harvard Journal on Legislation* 9: 628–55.

Dunn, Charles, and Samuel Gove. 1972. "Legislative Reform Vacuum: The Illinois Case." *National Civic Review* 61: 441–46.

Duverger, Maurice. 1954. *Political Parties.* New York: John Wiley.

Elkin, Stephen L. 1987. *City and Regime in the American Republic.* Chicago: University of Chicago Press.

Engstrom, Richard. 1990. "Cincinnati's 1988 Proportional Representation Initiative." *Electoral Studies* 9: 217–25.

———. 1993. "The Single-Transferable Vote: An Alternative Remedy for Minority Vote Dilution." *University of San Francisco Law Review* 27: 781–813.

———. 2000. Comments. Roundtable on Proportional Representation, annual meeting of the Western Political Science Association, San Jose, Calif., March 24–26.

Engstrom, R., and C. Barrilleaux. 1991. "Native Americans and Cumulative Voting: The Sisseton-Wahpeton Sioux." *Social Science Quarterly* 72: 388–93.

Engstrom, R., and M. McDonald. 1981. "The Election of Blacks to City Councils: Clarifying the Impact of Electoral Arrangements on the Seats/Population Relationship." *American Political Science Review* 75: 344–54.

Engstrom, Richard, Delbert Taebel, and Richard Cole. 1989. "Cumulative Voting as a Remedy for Minority Vote Dilution: The Case of Alamogordo, New Mexico." *Journal of Law and Politics* 5: 469–97.

Evans, James. 1996. *Straightforward Statistics for the Behavioral Sciences.* Pacific Grove, Calif.: Brooks/Cole.

Everson, David, Joan Parker, William Day, Rita Harmony, and Kent Redfield. 1982. "The Cutback Amendment: Illinois Special Issues Report." Springfield, Ill.: Sangamon State University.

Farrell, David. 1997. *Comparing Electoral Systems.* Englewood Cliffs, N.J.: Prentice Hall.

———. 2001. *Electoral Systems: A Comparative Introduction.* London: Palgrave.

Fishkin, James. 1991. *Democracy and Deliberation: New Directions for Democratic Reform.* New Haven, Conn.: Yale University Press.

Franklin, Mark, Richard G. Niemi, and Guy Whitten. 1992. "Constituency Characteristics, Individual Characteristics and Tactical Voting in the 1989 British General Election." *British Journal of Political Science* 22, no. 2 (April): 229–54.

Gallagher, M. 1996. "Intra-Party Competition at Irish Elections 1965–1994." Paper presented at the Conference on Elections in Australia, Ireland and Malta under STV, Laguna Beach, Calif., December 14–15.

Garvin, J. 1935. *The Life of Joseph Chamberlain.* London: Macmillan.

Garza v. County of Los Angeles, 918 F2d 763, 770–71 (9th Cir. 1990).

Gay, Claudine. 1997. "Taking Charge: Black Electoral Success and the Redefinition of American Politics." Ph.D. diss., Harvard University, Cambridge, Mass.

Gerber, Elizabeth, Rebecca Morton, and Thomas Rietz. 1998. "Minority Representation in Multimember Districts." *American Political Science Review* 92: 1127–44.

Gerstenberg, C. 1910. "The Mathematics of Cumulative Voting." *Journal of Accountancy* 9: 177–88.

Gilliam, Frank, and Karen Kaufmann. 1996. "Is there an Empowerment Life-Cycle?: Long-Term Black Empowerment and Its Impact on Voter Participation." Western Political Science Association, San Francisco, March 14–16.

Glasser, A. 1959. "Game Theory and Cumulative Voting." *Management Science* 5: 151–56.

Goldburg, C. 1994. "The Accuracy of Game Theory Predictions for Political Behavior: Cumulative Voting in Illinois Revisited." *Journal of Politics* 56: 885–900.

Gomez v. City of Watsonville, 863 F2d 1407, 1414 (9th Cir. 1988).

Grey, Earl. 1853. *The Colonial Policy of the Administration of Lord John Russell,* vol. 2 London: Bentley.

Grofman, Bernard. 1975. "A Review of Macro Election Systems." *Sozialwissenschaftliches Jahrbuch für Politik* 4: 303–52.

______. 1995. "*Shaw v. Reno* and the Future of the Voting Rights Act." *PS: Political Science and Politics* 28: 27–36.

Grofman, Bernard, and Chandler Davidson. 1992. *Controversies in Minority Voting: The Voting Rights Act in Perspective.* Washington, D.C.: Brookings Institute Press.

Grofman, Bernard, and Lisa Handley. 1989. "Minority Population and Black and Hispanic Congressional Success in the 1970s and 1980s." *American Politics Quarterly* 17: 436–45.

Grofman, Bernard, Lisa Handley, and Richard G. Niemi. 1992. *Minority Representation and the Quest for Voting Equality.* New York: Cambridge University Press.

Grofman, Bernard, and Arend Lijphart. 1986. *Electoral Laws and Their Political Consequences.* New York: Agathon Press.

Guinier, Lani. 1991. "No Two Seats: The Elusive Quest for Political Equality." *Virginia Law Review* 77: 1414–1514.

______. 1993. "Second Proms and Second Primaries: The Limits of Majority Rule." *National Civic Review* 82: 168–77.

______. 1994. *Tyranny of the Majority: Fundamental Fairness in Representative Democracy.* New York: Free Press.

______. 1998. *Lift Every Voice: Turning a Civil Rights Setback into a New Vision of Social Justice.* New York: Simon and Schuster.

Gunther, R. 1989. "Electoral Laws, Party Systems and Elites: The Case of Spain." *American Political Science Review* 83: 835–58.

Harrop, M., and W. Miller. 1987. *Elections and Voters: A Comparative Introduction.* Basingstoke: Macmillan Education.

Hays, Samuel. 1964. "The Politics of Municipal Reform in the Progressive Era." *Pacific Northwest Quarterly* 55: 157–69.

Helig, P., and R. Mundt. 1983. "Changes in Representation Equity: The Effect of Adopting Districts." *Social Science Quarterly* 64: 393–97.

Hill, Kim Q., and Jan Leighley. 1993. "Party, Ideology, Organization and Competitiveness as Mobilizing Forces in Gubernatorial Elections." *American Journal of Political Science* 37: 1158–78.

Horowitz, David. 1991. *A Democratic South Africa? Constitutional Engineering in a Divided Society.* Berkeley: University of California Press.

Humphreys, J. 1927. *Proportional Representation: A Study in Methods of Election.* London: Methuen.

Hyneman, C., and J. Margon. 1937. "Cumulative Voting in Illinois." *Illinois Law Review* 32: 12–31.

Jackman, Robert. 1987. "Political Institutions and Voter Turnout in the Industrial Democracies." *American Political Science Review* 81: 405–424.

Jackman, Robert, and Ross Miller. 1995. "Voter Turnout in the Industrial Democracies during the 1980s." *Comparative Political Studies* 27:467–92.

Jackson, Robert, Robert Brown, and Gerald Wright. 1998. "Registration, Turnout and the Electoral Representatives of U.S. State Electorates." *American Politics Quarterly* 26: 259–89.

Jenkins Report. 1998. The Report of the Independent Commission on the Voting System. HMSO London. Cm 4090-I; Cm 4090-II.

Jesse, E. 1988. "Split-Voting in the Federal Republic of Germany: An Analysis of the Federal Elections from 1953 to 1987." *Electoral Studies* 7: 109–24.

Johnson, R. 1979. *Political, Electoral and Spatial Systems.* New York: Oxford University Press.

Johnston, R., and J. Vowles. 1997. "The New Rules and the New Game in New Zealand Elections: Implications for the Campaign." Paper presented at the annual meeting of the American Political Science Association, Washington, D.C., August 29–September 2.

Karing, A., and S. Welch. 1978. *Black Representation and Urban Policy.* Chicago: University of Chicago Press.

Katz, Richard. 1981. "But How Many Candidates Should We Have in Donegal?" *British Journal of Political Science* 11: 117–22.

———. 1986. "Intraparty Preference Voting." In *Electoral Laws and Their Political Consequences,* edited by Bernard Grofman and Arend Lijphart. New York: Agathon Press.

———. 1996. "Electoral Reform and the Transformation of Party Politics in Italy." *Party Politics* 2: 31–53.

Keech, W., and Michael Sistrom. 1994. "North Carolina." In *Quiet Revolution in the South: The Impact of the Voting Rights Act,* edited by C. Davidson and B. Grofman. Princeton, N.J.: Princeton University Press.

Key, V. O. 1961. *Public Opinion and American Democracy.* New York: Knopf.

Kim, J., and C. W. Muller. 1978. *Factor Analysis: Statistical Methods and Practical Issues.* Beverly Hills, Calif.: Sage.

Kirk, R. E. 1995. *Experimental Design: Procedures for the Behavioral Sciences.* 3d ed. Pacific Grove, Calif.: Brooks/Cole.

Lakeman, Enid. 1974. *How Democracies Vote.* London: Faber and Faber.

Lanoue, David, and Shaun Bowler. 1992. "Sources of Tactical Voting in British Parliamentary Elections 1983–1987." *Political Behavior* 14: 141–57.

Leighley, Jan, and Jonathan Nagler. 1992. "Individual and Systemic Differences on Turnout: Who Votes? 1984." *Journal of Politics* 54: 635–717.

Lijphart, A. 1984. *Democracies: Patterns of Majoritarian and Consensus Government in Twenty-One Countries.* New Haven, Conn.: Yale University Press.

______. 1994. *Electoral Systems and Party Systems.* New York: Oxford University Press.

Lijphart, A., and B. Grofman. 1984. *Choosing an Electoral System.* New York: Praeger.

Lipset, S. M. 1960. "Party Systems and the Representation of Social Groups." *European Journal of Sociology* 1: 61–80.

Logan, John, and Harvey Molotch. 1987. *Urban Fortunes: The Political Economy of Place.* Berkeley: University of California Press.

Lublin, David. 1997. *The Paradox of Representation: Racial Gerrymandering and Minority Interests in Congress.* Princeton, N.J.: Princeton University Press.

Lublin, David, and Stephen Voss. 2000. "Racial Redistricting and Realignment in Southern State Legislatures." *American Journal of Political Science* 44, no. 4 (October): 792–810.

Lupia, Arthur, and Elizabeth Gerber. 1995. "Campaign Competition and Policy Responsiveness in Direct Legislation Elections." *Political Behavior* 17: 287–306.

MacManus, Susan A. 1995. "The Appropriateness of Biracial Approaches to Measuring Fairness of Representation in a Multicultural World." In "Symposium: The Voting Rights Act after Shaw v. Reno?" *PS: Political Science and Politics* 28, no. 1 (March): 42–47.

Manin, Bernard. 1997. *The Principles of Representative Government.* New York: Cambridge University Press.

Mansbridge, Jane. 1999. "Should Blacks Represent Blacks and Women Represent Women? A Contingent Yes." *Journal of Politics* 61: 628–57.

Massey, D., and Nancy D. 1987. "Trends in Residential Segregation of Blacks, Hispanics and Asians: 1970–80." *American Sociological Review* 52: 802–25.

Mayhew, D. 1974. *Congress: The Electoral Connection.* New Haven, Conn.: Yale University Press.

McCann, W. 1960. "Trade Unionist, Co-Operative and Socialist Organizations in Relation to Popular Education 1870–1902." Ph.D. diss., University of Manchester.

McCracken, J. 1967. *The Cape Parliament 1854–1910.* Oxford: Clarendon Press.

McLean, I. 1991. "Forms of Representation and Systems of Voting." In *Political Theory Today,* edited by David Held. Cambridge, England: Polity Press.

McLean, I., A. McMillan, and B. Monroe. 1996. *A Mathematical Approach to PR: Duncan Black on Lewis Carroll.* New York: Kluwer.

McMillan, A. 1997. "The Limited Vote in Britain: A Failed Attempt at PR." *Representation* 33, no. 3: 85–90.

Mill, John Stuart, 1861. *Considerations on Representative Government.* London: Parker, Son, and Bourn.

Miller v. Johnson, 515 US 900, 916 (1995).

Moncrief, Gary, Joel Thompson, and Karl Kurtz. 1996. "The Old Statehouse, It Ain't What It Used to Be." *Legislative Studies Quarterly* 21: 57–72.

Nagler, Jonathan. 1991. "The Effects of Registration Laws and Education on U.S. Voter Turnout." *American Political Science Review* 85: 1393–1406.

New Zealand Royal Commission on Electoral Reform. 1986. *Toward a Better Democracy.* Wellington: Government Printer.

Niemi, Richard, Guy Whitten, and Mark Franklin. 1991. "Constituency Characteristics, Individual Characteristics and Tactical Voting in the 1987 British General Election." Paper presented at the annual meeting of the American Political Science Association, Washington, D.C., August.

———. 1992. "Constituency Characteristics, Individual Characteristics and Tactical Voting in the 1987 British General Elections." *British Journal of Political Science* 23: 131–37.

Niemi, Richard G., Mark Franklin, and Guy Whitten. 1994. "The Two Faces of Tactical Voting." *British Journal of Political Science* 24, no. 4 (October): 549–57.

Ordeshook, Peter. 1992. *A Political Theory Primer.* New York: Routledge.

Overby, L. Marvin, and Kenneth M. Cosgrove. 1996. "Unintended Consequences? Racial Redistricting and the Representation of Minority Interests." *The Journal of Politics* 58, no. 2 (May): 540–50.

Palda, Filip. 1994. *How Much Is Your Vote Worth.* San Francisco: ICS Press.

Pateman, Carole. 1970. *Participation and Democratic Theory.* New York: Cambridge University Press.

Patterson, Samuel, and Gregory Caldeira. 1983. "Getting out the Vote: Participation in Gubernatorial Elections." *American Political Science Review* 77: 675–89.

Penncock, Roland. 1979. *Democratic Political Theory.* Princeton, N.J.: Princeton University Press.

Peterson, Paul. 1981. *City Limits.* Chicago: University of Chicago Press.

Pildes, Richard, and Kristen Donoghue. 1995. "Cumulative Voting in the United States." *University of Chicago Legal Forum,* 241–312.

Pildes, Richard, and Richard Niemi. 1993. "Expressive Harms, 'Bizarre Districts' and Voting Rights: Evaluating Election-District Appearances after *Shaw v Reno.*" *Michigan Law Review* 92: 483–587.

Pitkin, Hannah. 1967. *The Concept of Representation.* Berkeley: University of California Press.

Polinard, J., R. Wrinkle, and T. Longoria. 1991. "The Impact of District Elections on the Mexican American Community: The Electoral Perspective." *Social Science Quarterly* 72: 608–14.

Powell, G. Bingham, Jr. 1986. "American Voter Turnout in Comparative Perspective." *American Political Science Review* 80: 17–43.

Prewitt, Kenneth. 1970. *The Recruitment of Political Leaders: A Study of Citizen-Politicians.* New York: Bobbs-Merrill.

Rae, Douglas. 1971. *The Political Consequences of Electoral Laws.* New Haven, Conn.: Yale University Press.

Rae D., V. Hanby, and J. Loosemore. 1971. "Thresholds of Representation and Thresholds of Exclusion: An Analytic Note on Electoral Systems." *Comparative Political Studies* 3: 479–88.

Rausch, John David. 2001. "Cumulative Voting Comes to the Amarillo Independent School District: A Research Note." *Politics & Policy* 29, no. 4: 602–19.

Reapportionment Hearings. 1965. Assembly Committee on Elections and Reapportionment Records, LP 178, California State Archives, Sacramento, California.

Reeves, Keith. 1997. *Voting Hopes or Voting Fears: White Voters, Black Candidates and Racial Politics in America.* New York: Oxford University Press.

Reilly, Ben. "The Alternative Vote and Ethnic Accommodation: New Evidence from Papua New Guinea." *Electoral Studies* 16: 1–11.

Reno v. Bossier Parish School Board, 520 US 471 (1997).

Riker, William. 1982. "The Two-Party System and Duverger's Law: An Essay of the History of Political Science." *American Political Science Review* 76: 753–66.

Ritchie, R., and S. Hill. 1999. *Reflecting All of Us the Case for Proportional Representation.* Boston: Beacon Press.

Rosenstone, Steven. 1982. "Economic Adversity and Voter Turnout." *American Journal of Political Science* 26: 25–46.

Rosenstone, Steven J., and John Mark Hansen. 1993. *Mobilization, Participation, and Democracy in America.* New York: Macmillan.

Rosenstone, Steven, and Raymond Wolfinger. 1978. "The Effects of Registration Laws on Voter Turnout." *American Political Science Review* 72: 22–45.

Ross, J. F. 1955. *Elections and Electors.* London: Eyre and Spottiswoode.

Royal Commission on Electoral Systems. 1910. Cmd 5163. London: HMSO.

Rule, Wilma. 1992. "Multi-Member Districts: Minority and Anglo Women's and Men's Recruitment Opportunity." In *United States Electoral Systems: Their Impact on Women and Minorities,* edited by Wilma Rule and Joseph Zimmerman. New York: Greenwood Press.

Rule, Wilma, and Joseph Zimmerman. 1992. *United States Electoral Systems: Their Impact on Women and Minorities.* New York: Greenwood Press.

Rusk, Jerrold G. 1970. "The Effect of the Australian Ballot Reform on Split Ticket Voting: 1876–1908." *The American Political Science Review* 64, no. 4. (December): 1220–38.

Sass, Tim R., and Stephen Mehay. n.d. "Minority Representation, Election Method and Policy Influence." Unpublished manuscript, Department of Economics, Florida State University.

Sawyer, Jack, and Duncan MacRae. 1962. "Game Theory and Cumulative Voting in Illinois: 1902–1954." *American Political Science Review* 56: 936–46.

Schattschneider, E. E. 1942. *Party Government.* New York: Rinehart.

Shaffer, Stephen. 1981. "A Multivariate Explanation of Decreasing Turnout in Presidential Elections, 1960–76." *American Journal of Political Science* 25: 68–95.

Shaw v. Hunt, 116 SCt 1895, 1905 (1996).

Shaw v. Reno, 113 SCt 2816 (1993).

Shugart M., and M. Wattenberg. 2001. *Mixed-Member Electoral Systems: The Best of Both Worlds?* New York: Oxford University Press.

Silva, R. 1964. "Relation of Representation and the Party System to the Number of Seats Apportioned to a Legislative District." *Western Political Quarterly* 18: 742–69.

Stanley, H., and R. Niemi. 1995. "The Demise of the New Deal Coalition Partnership and Group Support 1952–1992." In *Democracy's Feast,* edited by Herbert Weisberg. Chatham, N.J.: Chatham House.

Still, E. 1984. "Alternatives to Single-Member Districts." In *Minority Vote Dilution,* edited by C. Davidson. Washington, D.C.: Howard University Press.

———. 1992. "Voluntary Constituencies: Modified At-Large Voting as a Remedy for Minority Vote Dilution in Judicial Elections." *Yale Law and Policy Journal* 9: 354–70.

Studlar, Donley, and Ian McAllister. 1994. "The Electoral Connection in Australia: Candidate Roles, Campaign Activity, and the Popular Vote." *Political Behavior* 16: 385–409.

Sutherland, G. 1973. *Policy Making in Elementary Education 1870–1895.* New York: Oxford University Press.

Swain, Carol. 1993. *Black Faces, Black Interests: The Representation of African Americans in Congress.* Cambridge, Mass.: Harvard University Press.

Taagepera, R., and M. Shugart. 1989. *Seats and Votes.* New Haven, Conn.: Yale University Press.

Taebel, D. 1978. "Minority Representation on City Councils: The Impact of Structure on Blacks and Hispanics." *Social Science Quarterly* 59: 142–52.

Taebel, D., Richard Engstrom, and Richard Cole. 1988. "Alternative Electoral Systems as Remedies for Minority Vote Dilution." *Hamline Journal of Public Law and Policy* 11: 19–29.

Tate, Katherine. 1994. *From Protest to Politics: The New Black Voters in American Elections.* Cambridge, Mass.: Harvard University Press.

Taylor, Charles. 1992. *Multiculturalism and the Politics of Recognition.* Princeton, N.J.: Princeton University Press.

Thernstrom, Abigail. 1987. *Whose Votes Count? Affirmative Action and Minority Voting Rights.* Cambridge, Mass.: Harvard University Press.

Thomas, J., and W. Stewart. 1988. *Alabama Government and Politics.* Lincoln: University of Nebraska Press.

Thornburg v. Gingles, 478 US 30, 48–49 (1986).

Trapido, S. 1964. "Origins of the Cape Franchise Qualification 1853." *Journal of African History* 20: 37–53.

Tsebelis, George. 1986. "A General Model of Tactical and Inverse Tactical Voting." *British Journal of Political Science* 16: 395–404.

Uhlaner, Carole, Bruce Cain, and Rod Kiewiet. 1989. "Political Participation of Ethnic Minorities." *Political Behavior* 11 (September): 195–231.

United Kingdom. Parliament. 1884–85. *Report and Minutes of Evidence of the Select Committee on School Board Voting.* Parliamentary Papers.

U.S. Census. 2000. Washington, D.C.: Department of Commerce, Bureau of the Census.

U.S. Civil Rights Commission. 1981. "The Voting Rights Act: Unfulfilled Goals."

Valadez, Jorge. 2001. Deliberative Democracy, Political Legitimacy and Self-Determination in Multicultural Societies. Boulder, Colo.: Westview Press.

Vanderleeuw, James, and Glenn Utter. 1993. "Voter Roll-off and the Electoral Context: A Test of Two Theses." *Social Science Quarterly* 74: 664–73.

Vedlitz, A., and C. Johnson. 1982. "Community Segregation, Electoral Structure and Minority Representation." *Social Science Quarterly* 67: 729–36.

Verba, Sidney. 1965. "Conclusion: Comparative Political Culture." In *Political*

Culture and Political Development, edited by Lucian Pye and Sidney Verba. Princeton, N.J.: Princeton University Press.

Verba, Sidney, and Norman Nie. 1972. *Participation in America: Political Democracy and Social Equality.* New York: Harper and Row.

Verba, Sidney, Norman Nie, and Jae-On Kim. 1978. *Participation and Political Equality: A Seven-Nation Comparison.* New York: Cambridge University Press.

Voting Rights Act of 1965. Pub. L. No. 89-110, 79 Stat. 437 (codified at 42 US §§ 1971–1973p) (1988).

Vowles, Jack, Peter Aimer, Susan Banducci, and Jeffrey Karp, eds. 1998. *Voters' Victory? New Zealand's First Election under Proportional Representation.* Aukland: Aukland University Press.

Weaver, Leon. 1984. "Semi-Proportional and Proportional Representation Systems in the United States." In *Choosing an Electoral System,* edited by A. Lijphart and B. Grofman. New York: Praeger.

———. 1986. "The Rise, Decline and Resurrection of Proportional Representation in Local Governments in the United States." In *Electoral Laws and Their Political Consequences,* edited by B. Grofman and A. Lijphart. New York: Agathon Press.

Welch, S. 1990. "The Impact of At-Large Elections on the Representation of Blacks and Hispanics." *Journal of Politics* 52: 1050–76.

Whitby, Kenny J. 1997. *The Color of Representation: Congressional Behavior and Black Interests.* Ann Arbor: University of Michigan Press.

Wiggins, Charles, and Janice Petty. 1979. "Cumulative Voting and Electoral Competition in the Illinois House." *American Politics Quarterly* 7: 345–65.

Will, George. 1992. *Restoration: Congress. Term Limits and the Recovery of Deliberative Democracy.* New York: Free Press.

Williams, Oliver P., and Charles Adrian. 1963. *Four Cities: A Study in Comparative Policy Making.* Philadelphia: University of Pennsylvania Press.

Wolfinger, Raymond E., and Steven J. Rosenstone. 1980. *Who Votes?* New Haven, Conn.: Yale University Press.

Zeller, Belle, and Hugh A. Bone. 1948. "American Government and Politics: The Repeal of PR in New York City—Ten Years in Retrospect." *American Political Science Review* 42, no. 6 (December 1948): 1127–48.

INDEX

African American representation: compared to Latino representation, 95–106; under CV, 108–112
Agee, Bobby, 21, 45
Alamogordo, New Mexico, 5, 21, 23, 46, 66, 67, 71, 72, 80
Allen v. Alabama State Elections Board, 15
Amarillo, Texas, 1, 4, 115
Amy, D., 20, 29, 77–78
Anderson, C., 7, 8
Aspin, L., 35
at-large districts: and minority representation, 92–94
at-large elections, 4, 14, 16–17, 26; compared to CV, 67–68; districts, 4
Atlanta, Texas, 48

ballot: sample, 24; structure, 28–29
Banducci, S., 7, 8
Barber, K., 14–15, 29
Barrilleaux, C., 22, 66, 67, 69
Birch, A., 9
Blair, G., 19,30
Blais, A., 7, 77
Bowler, S., 9, 28, 36
Brischetto, R., 22, 46, 48, 67, 72, 97
Buckalew, Senator C., 2, 27, 116
Bullock, C., 97, 200
Bush v. Vera, 17

campaign activity, 55–57, 57–61; across electoral systems, 53–54; candidate behavior, 34–35, 41–42, 44–46, 49–50; minority candidates, 44–46; types of (see also campaign spending), 52–55
campaign contact with voters, 69–73
campaign spending, 49–50; across electoral systems, 55–57; and informed voters, 55; and minorities, 55, 63
campaigns, 39, 57–61
candidates: activities, 44–46; campaigning, 44–46, 49–50; collusion and CV, 34–35; and coordination problem, 35–36; entry of, 41–42, 77–79; incentives for, 53–54; mobilization of, 39–46; pool, 39–40; and strategic demands of CV, 107; strategy and turnout, 75–76;
Cape Colony experience with CV, 19
categorical and preferential (ordinal) systems, 29
categorical voting, 28
Center for Voting and Democracy, 114
Chilton Co., Alabama, 21, 66, 73
Clovis, New Mexico, 80
comparative case approach, 51–52, 80–82
comparative method, 5–8
competition, lack of under SMSP, 53–55
consensus model, 4
coordination: and minorities, 43–44, 50; of voters, 32–36, 37–38, 43–46, 69–73
coordination problem and candidates, 42–43
coordination problems, 40, 42–43; facing candidates, 35–36; facing voters, 32–35; and political parties, 35–36; under CV, 27–28, 39–40, 32–35
Cox, G., 8, 32, 36, 79, 94
CV (cumulative voting): and African Americans, 108–112; comparison with other electoral systems, 25–27, 28–31; complexity of, 65–66; and coordination problems, 27–28, 32–35, 39–40; elections in practice, 23–28; history of, 14–15, 19–23; and Latinos, 103–6; and LV compared, 35, 75, 80–81; mechanical effect of , 28; as proportional system, 20; and SMSP compared, 23, 46–47; and voter registration, 47–48, 52–53; and voter turnout, 79–91;

D'Hondt, 26
Davidson, C., 4, 16, 43, 48
descriptive representation, 5–6, 10–11, 20, 107–107
district magnitude, 8, 78
districting, 77
Donoghue, K., 21, 22, 45, 55, 66
Donovan, T., 6, 8, 9, 36, 63

elections, winning, 9
electoral competition and electoral system, 52–55
electoral engineering, 63, 90, 113–115
electoral reform outside U.S., 6–8
electoral system and incentives to mobilize, 75–77
electoral systems compared, 25–30, 39, 62–63, 65–66
elite incentives, 8, 39, 53–54
endorsements, 44–49
Engstrom, R., 2, 4,14, 17, 21, 22, 35, 46, 66, 67, 72, 93, 97, 103, 104, 116

Farrell, D., 28, 29
Fishkin, J., 9
Fraga, L., 43, 48

Garza v. Los Angeles County, 16
Gerber, E., 32, 55
Goldburg, E., 34–35
Gomez v. Watsonville, 16
Grofman, B., 4, 15, 17, 18, 23, 25, 28
group campaigning on behalf of candidate, 46–49, 52
groups and campaigns, 61–63
Guin, Alabama, 23, 73
Guinier, L., 2, 5, 10, 18, 19, 20, 50, 77, 112, 114, 116, 117

Illinois state elections, 20, 34–35
incentives: to manage votes, 32–36, 37–38, 43–46, 69–73; to mobilize voters, 75–77; of political elites, 8, 39

institutional design, 63, 90–91, 113–15

Jackman, R., 7, 77
Jenkins Report, 9

Karp, J., 7, 8
Katz, R., 6

Lakeman, E., 20, 94
Latino representation: and African American representation compared, 95–106; under CV, 103–6
Lijphart, A., 4, 7, 36, 77
List PR, 29
Lublin, D., 4, 17, 18
LULAC, 21, 43, 47
LV (limited voting), 36, 37; compared to CV, 35, 80

MacRae, D., 34
majoritarian systems, 114
majority-minority districts, 4–5, 10, 15–17, 90; criticisms of, 17–18
Mansbridge, D., 10
methodology, 51–52, 94–95, 97. *See also* research design
Mill, J. S., 9, 27
Miller v. Johnson, 17
minorities and turnout, 83–84
minority candidates: activity compared, 44–46; campaigning, 48–49, 69; plumping, 44–49
minority representation, 3–6, 92–94, 108–112
minority voters and complexity of CV, 67–73
Moncada, Inez, 21, 46, 72
Morton, Texas, 40, 48
multimember districts, 78–79

NAACP, 43
New Zealand Royal Commission, 9
nomination, 32–34, 35–36, 37–38, 50. *See also* overnomination
nonpartisan elections, and CV, 42–43
novelty effect, 54, 89

ordinal systems, 37, 39, 65; advantages of, 117–19. *See also* preferential systems
outcome versus process, 6, 8–9, 36–37
overnomination, 34–36, 37–38, 50. *See also* nomination.

Pateman, C., 9
Peoria, Illinois, 5, 7, 23, 41–42, 71–72, 73, 80, 113
Pildes, R., 21, 22, 45, 55, 66
Pitkin, H., 9
plumping, 33, 34, 67, 68; and candidate strategy, 44–46, 49; and candidates, 69–70, 75; and coordination, 33; and minority candidates, 49; as campaign appeal, 46; by minority voters, 70–73
political parties: and strategic demands of CV, 107; as solution to coordination problems, 35–36, 40, 42–43
Populists and Progressives, 14–15
preferential and categorical voting compared, 29
preferential systems, 29–30, 117–19; compared to categorical voting (*see also* ordinal voting), 29
process versus outcome, 6, 8–9, 36–37
proportional representation (PR): and turnout, 77–79; as a remedy for minority underrepresentation, 29; efficacy under, 8, 9, 108–112
proportionality, 8; of CV, 35

Rae, D., 28, 33, 34
Rausch, D., 4
Reno v. Bossier Parish School Board, 18
Report of the Committee of the Board of Trade, 19
representation, 92–93, 107–8
research design, 5–8, 43–46, 51–52, 80–82, 92–93, 94–95, 97, 123–26
Royal Commission, 66
Rule, W., 14

Sawyer, M., 34
school board elections in Victorian England, 19–20
seats-population relationship, 93–106; for minorities, 98–106
second-order elections, 6
Shaw v. Hunt, 17
Shaw v. Reno, 5, 17, 13
Shugart, M., 36
single non-transferable vote (SNTV), 36
single transferable vote (STV), 14–15, 28–29, 30, 65, 114, 117–19
Sisseton, South Dakota, 67–73, 113
slating organizations, 43, 44; and CV campaigns, 46–49, 52, 61–63
Still, E., 18, 20, 35, 36, 65, 77
strategic demands, 107; of CV, 32–36, 65–70; of CV and LV, 35. *See also* incentives
Swain, C., 18

Taagepera, R., 36
Taebel, D., 21, 22
Thernstrom, A., 77
Thornburg v. Gingles, 4, 5, 16
threshold of exclusion, 25, 26–27, 40–41, 75
threshold of representation, 40–41, 25, 26–27, 78
trade-offs in institutional design, 90–91

U.S. population diversity, 2,4,5
U.S. Supreme Court, 16–18

vote management, 32–36, 37–38, 43–48, 50, 69–73
voter coordination, strategies of, 43–46
voter mobilization, 46–48, 75–91
voter registration: and CV, 47–48, 52–53; and mobilization, 46–48
voter response to mobilization efforts, 73–74
voter turnout, 75–91; and candidate strategy, 75–76; and PR, 77–79, 90; by minorities, 83–84; under CV, 79–91
voters and complexity of CV, 67–73
votes, distribution of, 32–36, 37–38, 43–46, 69–73; wasted 37–38, 77
Voting Rights Act, 15–16, 93
Vowles, J., 6